THE EXCITEMENT OF BEGINNING

Whether we're looking forward to an upcoming vacation or the start of a new job—we all know the feeling of anticipation. We're not quite sure what lies ahead . . . but it promises to be good, and we're eager to start.

That's what the early Christians felt as they began the Great Adventure—their new life as followers of "the Way" they had learned from Jesus Christ, now returned to Heaven. In this second New Testament book in the **Bible Alive Series,** you can probe the first half of the Acts of the Apostles and the early Epistles of James, Galatians, and Romans You'll meet the people and grasp the teachings that made the early church the most dynamic movement the world has ever seen.

And with them . . . you too can go adventuring!

Other BIBLE ALIVE titles:

OLD TESTAMENT SURVEYS

Let Day Begin
Freedom Road
Years of Darkness, Days of Glory
Edge of Judgment
Lift High the Torch
Springtime Coming

NEW TESTAMENT SURVEYS

The Servant King
Regions Beyond
Christ Preeminent
Pass It On
His Glory

LARRY RICHARDS
BIBLE ALIVE SERIES

The Great Adventure

The First Days of the Church

Studies in Acts, James, Galatians, and Romans

David C. Cook Publishing Co.
ELGIN, ILLINOIS—WESTON, ONTARIO
LA HABRA, CALIFORNIA

THE GREAT ADVENTURE
© 1977 David C. Cook Publishing Co.

Scripture quotations, unless otherwise noted, are from the New International Version.

Published by David C. Cook Publishing Co., 850 N. Grove Ave., Elgin, IL 60120
Printed in the United States of America

ISBN 0-89191-053-0

CONTENTS

THE GREAT
ADVENTURE

THE GREAT ADVENTURE

I REMEMBER VERY CLEARLY walking with five-year-old Paul the day he started kindergarten in Dallas, Texas. He was proud and excited: his first day at school! How grown-up he felt, and how grown-up and confident he looked. He was taking an important step toward life's adventure.

Now, as I write this, Paul is talking of another step. He's about to go to Seattle to work with an art center established by Trinity Church. How grown-up he is. And how close to leaving home, establishing a separate identity, and working out the private destiny God has in store for him.

Each of us comes to a time like this. And many of us live to see our children reach out on their own. For both parent and child there's a strange mixture of excitement and loss. A whole phase of our life is being left behind. We move out, sad, and yet somehow happy, to meet the unknown.

It must have been very much like this for both Jesus and the disciples after His Resurrection.

Their years together were gone now. The agony

of the cross was past, swallowed up in the joy of the Resurrection. During the forty days after the Resurrection, as Jesus still met with the disciples, both the Lord and the Eleven must have been torn. Both knew the disciples would soon be launched on the greatest adventure the world has ever known, stepping out into the unknown to share Jesus with their whole world. They may have desperately wanted Jesus to remain with them. Yet, deep inside, the disciples knew that they had been prepared for just this mission. They stood poised, hesitating, and yet eager to move on.

THE NEW DAY

While the faith of Israel served as a foundation for the new faith about to break upon a world unaware, the months and years and decades ahead were unknown to the disciples. The Old Testament had been written and the faith of Israel revealed in a slow though sometimes tumultuous process across centuries of time. But now the promised Messiah of the Old Testament had broken into history. His presence and His teachings jolted the leaders of the Jews into violent resistance. Because He seemed a threat to all that they held dear (especially their own status and position), they refused to see Him as the fulfillment of man's hope. Rather than accept Christ, and with Him accept change, they fought against Jesus in desperate rebellion. Finally they seemed to triumph. Jesus' back was beaten with whips, His head crowned with thorns, and His torn

10

frame spiked to a wooden cross.

He died.

And even those who knew Him best thought it was the end.

Yet, with the third day's dawn, the jolting reality of the Resurrection began to quicken the disciples. With each appearance of the risen Jesus, the realization grew that the universe itself had reached a fork in the road, and a new direction had been set.

The disciples did not yet know what it meant or where that new direction would take them. But they sensed that the time had come. Jesus would leave them. And in His name they would venture out to begin the greatest adventure of all.

While it had taken some 1,100 years to record the Old Testament revelation, the New Testament would be completed in less than six decades. During these exciting years, old patterns of life and thought would be swept away or revitalized, and a new faith and life-style would emerge, formed around the person of Jesus Himself. The shadowy images of the old would take on a new and surprising shape in the light cast by God's revelation of Himself in Jesus. As Jesus had foretold, the new wine required new wineskins; the fulfilled elements of Old Testament times would find new form in the New.

And the great adventure meant more than just reshaping Israel. Jesus came as the door through whom all men might approach God. The disciples would be called on to confront the pagan cultures as well as Israel's culture. In their battle to reshape these worlds, men like Paul and Peter and James and

11

John would write inspired letters through which God has been guiding the believers of every ensuing age in a timeless conflict between God's Kingdom and the kingdoms of this world. In these New Testament letters, shaped as the early church first went adventuring, God continues to call men and women to experience personally the greatest adventure of them all.

At times we lose sight of the fact that the New Testament is God's invitation to us to go adventuring with Him today. Perhaps the words sound too familiar to us. We lose sight of the challenge and the joy of discovery reflected there. But we can recapture the excitement. We can find in the words and teachings of the New Testament God's own guidance for reshaping our lives. We can find guidance toward the mature, victorious, and adventurous life that we look to so longingly—and with such uncertainty. That new life, rich with its new wine and prepared in its new wineskins, is held out to us now as we go on into the New Testament pages we're about to explore.

A NEW FOCUS
Acts 1

While an invitation to adventure attracts us, it also makes us hesitate. Usually we're comfortable in familiar surroundings and situations. Even when we're uncomfortable, the uncertainty of an invitation into new and perhaps threatening circumstances isn't always accepted with delight.

We can see this same hesitancy in the disciples. For forty days, the Bible tells us, Jesus spoke with them about His Father's intention to build His own Kingdom in man's world. Jesus also encouraged His disciples: "Wait for the gift my Father promised, ... in a few days you will be baptized with the Holy Spirit" (Acts 1: 4, 5). Jesus did not push His followers unprepared into an adventure too great for them; He reminded them that He had promised them power. Even so, the disciples still looked longingly at the old patterns of thought and life. "Lord," they asked, "are you at this time going to restore the kingdom to Israel?" (Acts 1: 6).

This was a revealing and an important question. The Old Testament had foretold Jesus' coming, but the dominant impression the Jews had received was of His coming to be their King. They had visions of the Messiah rescuing them from Gentile dominion and giving them the exalted political and military position promised by the Old Testament prophets. Jesus' death had been doubly shocking to His followers. Not only had they loved Him, but they had also firmly expected Him to crush Rome's political and military power and to establish Israel as the dominant world power.

The believing Jew in Old Testament times knew that God rules over the whole world of men. Therefore, His sovereignty over history itself was recognized. But the Old Testament saint longed for the day when the hidden authority of Jehovah would be revealed to all, when the Lord's Messiah ("anointed king") would rule *visibly* over the world of men. So

13

even the twelve who were closest to Jesus were somewhat disappointed as He continued to teach and preach and heal instead of confronting the Roman empire.

Jesus had gently taught His followers that the Old Testament also spoke of the Messiah suffering and dying for man's sins. Christ's ministry was leading Him to a cross rather than a crown. But up to the very end the disciples still had visions of their Camelot: a new Jerusalem, with Jesus (and themselves) ruling the world. The death of Jesus had crushed that hope momentarily. But when Jesus arose, the vision of power and glory again caught and held their imagination. "Are you *at this time* going to restore the kingdom to Israel?" clearly reflects their longing for the life they had dreamed of for so many years.

Jesus' answer was gentle (Acts 1: 7, 8). First He pointed out that the prophesied Kingdom would come, but that its coming was *distant* rather than "at this time." God will keep His promises, and this world will know Jesus' rule. But for now life is to have a different focus for Jesus' followers. That focus, stated in utmost simplicity, is this: "You will be my witnesses." Jesus Himself is the focus, the center, of the believer's life. The meaning of our life, the reason that our life on earth can become a great adventure, is summed up in the fact that Jesus is real and that every action of our life can be a clear demonstration of the vital impact of the living God on human experience!

This was something the disciples had not yet

grasped but soon would. Jesus, living within them, would Himself transform their experience. Then everything they were as individuals and as a community would witness to His presence.

These words, "You will be my witnesses," were the last ones Jesus spoke to the Eleven. As a silent crowd of disciples watched, Jesus rose up, soaring away until the clouds hid Him from sight. Two angelic messengers completed Christ's answer to the earlier question: "This same Jesus, who has been taken from you into heaven, will come back in the same way you have seen him go into heaven" (Acts 1:11). This present time, during which the focus of our lives and the heart of our great adventure with God is summed up in Jesus, will come to an end, just as the Old Testament days came to an end in the cross. Only the end of *our* age will come with the return of Jesus Christ Himself, a return to set up the promised earthly Kingdom of the Old Testament.

That day will come. But, for now . . . for now the disciples turned away from the Mount of Ascension and returned to Jerusalem to wait for the promised power. They waited in prayer for the great adventure to break upon them and to catch them up in a joy and reality they still could not even begin to imagine.

THE DAY
Acts 2:1-21

The days of waiting passed (Acts 1:12-26). The little company of believers, numbering about 120, met daily. On one of these days, they chose Matthias to take the office which Judas had abandoned by his betrayal of Jesus. Judas, overcome with remorse and yet unwilling to turn to Jesus for pardon, had thrown the thirty pieces of silver for which he had betrayed the Lord down on the Temple floor and, rushing out, hanged himself.

Now another must take his office as an apostle. Searching among those who had been with Jesus since the beginning of His ministry and who had also been witnesses to the Resurrection, the little company found two candidates. Following an Old Testament practice, they then let God choose between the two by casting lots (much like our drawing of straws).

The company of the apostles was thus returned to its original twelve.

Apostles. This word *apostle* means "one sent out." In secular Greek it often referred to a ship or naval force sent on an expedition, seldom to an individual. Yet the word was chosen by Jewish translators of the Old Testament to reflect a Hebrew word referring to someone who acted as a representative for another.

In the New Testament the word is found ten times in the Gospels, twenty-eight times in Acts, and thirty-eight times in the Epistles, usually referring to men appointed by Christ for a special function in the church. While these men are primarily the Twelve and Paul, others are also called apostles.

There is no doubt that the apostles were given special authority and power. Not only were they witnesses to the events of Jesus' life but they were also authoritative interpreters of those events. As the body of apostolic teaching grew, it became clear that the Church was being "built upon the foundation of the apostles and prophets" (Eph. 2:20).

There is no indication in Scripture that the loyal apostles were replaced by others as they died (cf. Acts 12:2). As witnesses and interpreters of the purposes of God in the early days of the Church, the apostles stand unique. But as witnesses to the reality of Jesus, the apostles were about to enter into an adventure they share with all disciples of every age. And then the day arrived.

Pentecost (Acts 2:1). The Feast of Pentecost was one of the three annual Old Testament celebrations during which the men of Israel came to Jerusalem to worship at the Temple. It was a time when Jews from around the world gathered in their ancient homeland and offered sacrifice to the God of Abraham and Isaac and Jacob.

Pentecost was a harvest festival, coming at the time of the grain harvest, just fifty days after Passover. Each year the firstfruits of the harvest were offered with joy and thanksgiving, accompanied by the recitation of Deuteronomy 26:3-10 by the worshiper.

Pentecost was clearly God's choice time for the initiation of Jesus' followers into their great adventure. Just fifty days before, Jesus Himself had been crucified—and raised again. Now, as an indication of the great harvest of everlasting life that Jesus' death had won, the 120 believers were about to be touched by the Holy Spirit. They were to be the first of a vast multitude, the first of millions upon millions who would follow them into a unique relationship with God through Jesus Christ.

The choice of Pentecost was also an indication of the meaning of that new relationship for believers. The first words the Old Testament worshiper uttered at the Pentecost service were these:

> I declare this day to the Lord your God that I have come into the land which the Lord swore to our fathers to give us.
>
> *Deuteronomy 26:3* (RSV)

I declare that I have entered in! This is just what Pentecost meant to the first disciples, and what it should mean to us. Through Jesus, we have entered into everything the Promised Land foreshadowed; we are now free to experience the fullness of all the good things the Lord our God has chosen to give men.

And God's first gift was the gift of the Holy Spirit.

The Holy Spirit (Acts 2:2-21). The Bible speaks of the Holy Spirit as a person, an individual distinct from and yet one with the Father and Son. As God, the Holy Spirit had various relationships with men in Old Testament times. But the Old Testament also spoke of a coming day when God would enter into a new and special relationship with men. Jesus also had spoken of this often. He looked forward to a time when He would be back with the Father, and the Spirit "whom those who believed in him were later to receive" would be given (Jn. 7:39). The

18

promised Spirit was to teach and guide believers (Jn. 14, 16) and, according to Jesus' final promise, to bring power for that new kind of life which witnesses to Jesus' reality (Acts 1: 8). In that day, Jesus had said, the Spirit would not simply be "with" the disciples, but "in" them (Jn. 14: 17)!

And Pentecost was the promised day!

The Bible tells us that His coming into believers was unmistakably marked. A mighty wind seemed to rush through the room where the 120 gathered; flames of fire flickered over each head; and as the Spirit filled them, individuals began to speak in languages they did not know.

This drew a great crowd of the men who had come to Jerusalem for the Pentecost festival. Each person heard the disciples speaking in the language of the land where he was presently living. "How is it," wondered the visitors, "that each of us hears them in his own native language? . . . We hear them declaring the wonders of God in our own tongues." (Acts 2: 8, 11). Perplexed and amazed, they asked each other, "What does this mean?" (vs. 12).

All too often that same question is asked today— without listening to Peter's response to those first questioners. All too often the answer given is designed to argue for or against the existence of this special gift of "tongues" in our own day. Whatever our opinion might be as to whether God still gives believers this gift,* the important point underlined

---

* The Bible's teaching on spiritual gifts is part of our study of I Corinthians, found in *Regions Beyond*, the third New Testament book of the **Bible Alive** Series.

by the Pentecost events is that now, at last, the Holy Spirit *is* given!

And this was Peter's answer to the men who demanded an explanation of the disciples: "This is what was spoken by the prophet Joel:

In the last days, God says, I will pour out my Spirit on all people.

Acts 2:16, 17

That great gift which God had reserved till the last days was being poured out freely now. All were to know the touch of the Spirit of God; both daughters and sons would be empowered by Him. Most significant of all, in that day in which the Spirit of God would flow out to touch and fill God's own, "everyone who calls on the name of the Lord will be saved" (Acts 2:21).

God was moving out beyond the boundaries of Israel to offer to *all* people that relationship with Himself which is at the heart of life's greatest adventure.

The disciples themselves didn't understand just then all that the Spirit's coming meant. They didn't see Pentecost as the beginning of the Church, as it later came to be understood. They did not realize that the Holy Spirit, living in each believer, would Himself constitute a living link binding each individual to other believers to form a vital, loving community.

But they did know that God's new day was *now*. They did know that the Holy Spirit had filled them

20

with Jesus' promised power. And they did begin, immediately, to explain the striking witness that the rushing wind and flames and tongues had given to every observer of the reality of God's presence in these set-apart men.

THE MESSAGE
Acts 2:22–3:26

Jesus' last instructions had been to focus on Himself: "You will be my witnesses" (Acts 1:8). Acts 2 and 3 show how clearly the early disciples maintained that focus. The two sermons of Peter recorded here give us a clear picture of the apostolic message and the very heart of the Gospel.

What were the basic elements of the apostolic preaching?

1. *Jesus, the historical person.* In each sermon Peter begins by confronting his hearers with the person who had lived among them: who was born, lived, performed His wonders and taught in our space and time, "as you yourselves know" (2:22). This was no mythical person, no invention of disciples parlaying the ignorance of gullible crowds into the beginnings of a new religion. Everyone knew Jesus. He had been a public figure, a chief topic of conversation for at least three years. Just fifty days before, He had been executed at the insistence of the Jewish leaders, with crowds of the common people shouting for His blood. Peter's words, "as you yourselves know," make it very clear that the Gospel is firmly rooted in historical reality.

21

And all Peter's hearers knew perfectly well who the historical Jesus was.

2. *Crucified.* A second element of the apostolic preaching involved confronting the hearers with the Crucifixion of Jesus, and even confronting them with their own guilt: "you put him to death by nailing him to the cross" (2: 23).

3. *Raised.* A third element also involves the statement of historical fact: Jesus was loosed from death's bonds and raised up by God, and "we all are witnesses of the fact" (2: 32).

4. *Correspondence with Old Testament prophecy.* Peter then goes on to point out that each of these historical events happened as God had foretold in the Old Testament. Rather than being a threat to the integrity of God's Word, Jesus and the events of His life and death and new life are foretold there. What Peter proclaims is in fullest harmony with God's total revelation.

5. *The promised Messiah.* Peter now goes on to interpret the facts he has laid out for his hearers. "Be assured of this: God has made this Jesus whom you crucified both Lord and Christ" (2: 36).

The conclusion is so clearly correct that his hearers are "cut to the heart" and beg the apostles, "Brothers, what shall we do?" (2: 37). This question leads into the last element of the apostolic preaching.

6. *Repentance and faith.* The word *repent* is a military term meaning to make an about-face. The men to whom Peter spoke had refused to accept Jesus as Lord and Messiah. They had hesitated, then pas-

sively participated in His execution. Now they were asked to make a clear-cut commitment and symbolize their response of faith by public baptism. What would be the result? All that Jesus' death and resurrection promised would be theirs: full forgiveness of sins and the gift of the Holy Spirit. The God they had scorned would welcome even them and, entering into their lives, fill them with power to launch out on life's great adventure.

So "Those who accepted his message were baptized," the text tells us, "and about three thousand were added to their number that day" (2:41).

How vital and contemporary these messages are even today. You and I have been invited by God to enter a living relationship with the historical Jesus. The Son of God lived and died and was raised again, all in accordance with the Scripture, that He might *today* bring forgiveness and power for a new life to all who respond to Him as Lord and Christ. He will be with us, as He was with the first disciples. His Holy Spirit will fill us, charging us with the power we need to live in God's new way.

GOING DEEPER

Here are some research and thought questions to help you explore the relationship of this passage to your life and to probe more deeply into its teachings.

to personalize

1. What does the word *adventure* bring to your mind? Describe something that you feel might be an adventure.

2. The author suggests that, in the New Testament, God invites us to seek out an adventure with Him and experience exciting growth and change. What aspect of your life do you think such an adventure would most likely affect?

3. Do you consider yourself an adventurous person? Do you think the early disciples (Acts 1) were adventurous persons? Why or why not?

4. From your study of Acts 2, what difference do you think the coming of the Holy Spirit to fill the disciples made? What similar differences do you think the Holy Spirit is to make in our lives today?

5. Examine carefully Peter's sermons in Acts 2 and 3, writing down the verses and phrases from each that fit the five elements of apostolic preaching which the author points out on pages 21, 22. Which of these seems most important today for a contemporary understanding of the Gospel? Why?

to probe

1. The author notes that Pentecost was purposely chosen by God for the Spirit's coming, and significantly so. What else can you discover in the Old Testament or New Testament about the day of Pentecost that suggests why it was the chosen day?

2. The Holy Spirit's coming described in Acts 2 is *the* significant mark of God's beginning something new—the Church. What does the Bible say about who the Holy Spirit is? What does He *do*? That is, what especially are His ministries? Use a concordance (or a theology text), and write a three- to five-page summary statement.

COMMUNITY

WHEN FRANK ACCEPTED CHRIST as his Savior, his parents saw his conversion as a denial of their family religion. At first they argued and ridiculed. Then, as they sensed the depth of their teenager's experience with Jesus, they increased the pressure. They offered Frank that set of expensive drums he'd wanted if only he'd give up this nonsense! Finally, the Leparises locked their son out of their home. If he would not remain true to the family faith, he would be cut off.

The first exciting days of the Church saw many experiences similar to Frank's as growth and change led to opposition. The contagious enthusiasm of those who believed in Jesus threatened the secure foundations of many people's religious convictions, and uneasy tolerance gave way to hostility. It was then that the little company of believers began to realize that the Church was a new community, a community of men and women who can be closer

25

than any family and who can provide the kind of loving support that believers then—and believers now, like Frank (whom I knew in our days together in a little Brooklyn, New York, church)—will always need.

Opposition to the message of a living Christ formed quickly. Peter's sermon, stimulated by the healing of the lame man (Acts 3), was only one instance of the disciples "teaching the people and proclaiming in Jesus the resurrection of the dead" (Acts 4:2). Soon some 5,000 men had joined the company of the committed. An annoyed clique of rulers and elders acted. They arrested Peter and John.

The confrontation (Acts 4:5-22). Called before the ruling body of Judaism, the apostles were questioned about the miracle of healing which Peter had performed. Boldly, Peter responded. The miracle had been performed "by the name of Jesus Christ of Nazareth, whom you crucified but whom God raised from the dead" (vs. 10). Only in Jesus, Peter went on to affirm, could salvation be found; there is no other name or way.

Such boldness from uneducated and common men stunned the elite group. Setting the apostles outside, the council conferred. There was no way to deny the public healing. Compromising, the rulers called Peter and John back and commanded them to stop all this talk of Jesus. Again speaking boldly, the two believers insisted that they would obey God rather than men. The frustrated rulers, unable to justify to the people any punishment of Peter and

John, threatened them and then let them go.

The fellowship of prayer (Acts 4:23-31). At this point in time we are introduced to one of the most significant dimensions of the new community's life. Peter and John immediately "went back to their own people and reported" (4:23). In the brotherhood of the church, Peter and John found others who cared and with whom they could share. Immediately the whole company accepted the burden of the two as their own and went to God in prayer.

Frank had many burdens to share with us back in Brooklyn. There was tremendous pain for him, and often that pain brought tears. But he had Christian friends who cared—friends who would listen, who would encourage, and who joined with him in prayer. Frank discovered as a young Christian what the early church learned in those first adventurous days. *A Christian is never alone.* Not only has the risen Christ sent the Holy Spirit to be with us, but He has also knit us together in a new community of fellowship and love.

This is one of the most important things we can learn as we begin our exploration of the New Testament. In the Scripture we see portrayed a church in which those touched by Christ discover a new capacity to love and care for one another. The church is more than a group of people who agree in their beliefs. The church is a family of brothers and sisters who experience the reality of Jesus' presence in and through their growing love for one another (cf. Jn. 13:33, 34). While some today have not tasted of that reality, this *is* a real and vital dimension of

27

Christian experience. And God invites each one of us to reach out and to know this touch of fellowship.

The text of Acts reports that as they prayed together, "they were all filled with the Holy Spirit and spoke the word of God boldly" (4:31). In the fellowship of prayer, God's power is poured again into our lives.

With one accord (Acts 4:32-37). This is a passage that has captured the imagination of Christians across the ages. "All the believers were one in heart and mind" (vs. 32). Growing together, the early church experienced a unique unity. Possessions were sold by the rich, and the proceeds were distributed to the poor. The sense of oneness was so great that no selfish hesitation kept anyone from reaching out to meet another's need. Because concern for the brothers outweighed the value of material possessions, love's expression was both practical and free. "There were no needy persons among them" (vs. 34).

This early evidence of the reality of Christian community is not necessarily a standard for the church today. But it is not as unusual as we may think. In our own local church just this kind of expression of love often takes place. Yet, the impact of the passage is not to promote some form of "Christian communism" but, rather, to highlight the truth of the writer's statement, "All the believers were one in heart and mind."

We are called to oneness in this Christian adventure. Oneness with our brothers and sisters frees us to share ourselves with each other, to support each

28

other in prayer, and to express love in many vital and practical ways.

Homothumadon: One Accord. A unique Greek word, used ten of its eleven New Testament occurrences in the Book of Acts, helps us understand the uniqueness of Christian community. *Homothumadon* is a compound of two words meaning to "rush along" and "in unison." The image is almost musical; a number of notes are sounded which, while different, harmonize in pitch and tone. As the instruments of a great orchestra blend under the direction of a concertmaster, so the Holy Spirit blends together the lives of members of Christ's church.

The first use of *homothumadon* is found in Acts 1:14. There, in the Upper Room, the eleven disciples and a few women are united in prayer. Earlier strife and jealousies are gone; the disciples are one, waiting for the Spirit's promised coming. Then in Acts 2:1 we see 120 believers gathered, focusing together on the Lord as they sense the Spirit's first dynamic touch. The next occurrence is Acts 2:46 (KJV), as the community (then some 3,000), "continuing daily with one accord [*homothumadon*] in the temple, and breaking bread from house to house, did eat their meat with gladness and singleness of heart." Again in 4:24 (KJV) we see the whole company, moved by Peter and John's report, as they "lifted up their voice to God with one accord." As those who are Jesus' own make Him the common focus of their lives and seek to help each other find the Holy Spirit's freedom in their lives, *homothumadon* becomes the mark of Christian community.

29

Sometimes we look back on these early chapters of Acts as though they pictured a Church that has been lost—as though unity and love and the experience of Jesus' presence are things that can never be ours. All too often we look back with longing because we have not yet experienced in our local church these things which are the mark of the Church. Let's not misunderstand. God's Spirit is still a present reality. *Homothumadon* is still possible in today's shattered and impersonal world. If we look for a reason for emptiness in our own experience, let's look first to the loss of our sense of Christian adventure. Or look to our hesitancy to share ourselves with our brothers and sisters. Or look to our failure to let others pick up the burdens of our lives and bring them in confident prayer to God.

The Church, the new community of God, *is* here today. *We are the Church,* and God the Spirit is able to take our 11s, and our 120s and our 3,000s and, as we joyfully focus our shared life on Jesus, orchestrate our lives to His wondrous "one accord."

JAMES

The church we see portrayed in the early chapters of Acts was both typical of what the Church is to be, and yet different.

At first the Jewish people viewed Christianity as a sect, as much an expression of Judaism as Sadduceeism, Pharisaism, a little angry band of Zealots, or the withdrawn Essenes. Recognized and named "the Way," the Christian community took part in the life and culture of Judea, worshiped at the Temple as did the others, and maintained the lifelong patterns of obedience to the Law.

It is in this context that the first of the New Testament letters was penned. Later sharp distinctions would occur between Christians and Jewish doctrine and practice. Later would come the exploration of the meaning of a faith that reaches out to encompass the Gentile as well as the Jew. None of this is found in the Book of James. Instead of emphasizing salvation by faith, James presupposes the apostolic teaching we have seen in Acts 2 and 3 and emphasizes the life of faith that followers of "the Way" are encouraged to live.

Looking into James's book we see another dimension of the early church's life. It was no easier to live a life of faith and *homothumadon* then than now! In that time, as in ours, the full expression of all that Jesus' presence with us means had to be worked out. Our adventure involves both a growing confidence in God and a growing willingness to bring all of life under the control of this Jesus who is the focus of our life.

James. The writer of the book is not James the brother of John, whose martyrdom under Herod Agrippa is reported in Acts 12:1-3. Instead, it is James, the oldest of Jesus' own brothers (see Mt. 13:55; Mk. 6:3). Although he was unresponsive during Jesus' earthly life (Jn. 7:5), James's faith seems to have come quickly after the Resurrection. Soon James, who also met the risen Christ (I Cor. 15:7), took leadership in the Jerusalem church.

31

Three years after Paul's conversion, this apostle to the Gentiles met James in Jerusalem (Gal. 1:19) at the first council of the church reported in Acts 15. It is James's summary that determines the decision of the whole body.

There is a great deal of tradition about James. Early Christian historians report that he was called "the Just." They picture him as a deeply pious man who lived in such holiness that he maintained the respect even of nonbelieving Jews.

James wrote his letter from Jerusalem, probably about A.D. 45-48. He wrote to Hebrew believers like himself, who may have been driven from Jerusalem and Judea by early persecutions. In his letter, James encourages Hebrew Christians to continue to live a life of holiness and trust, one which expresses the reality of Jesus in simple and practical ways.

This short letter, then, gives us added insight into the early days of the church: days of excitement and unity, yet days like our own when believers must learn to live in new ways. Looking into the Epistle of James, we're launched immediately into an exploration of what it meant to the early church to practice Christianity's living faith.

Faith's Personal Impact (Jas. 1:2-18). James immediately confronts his readers with a number of practical implications of the life of faith.

James 1:2-4. The pressures and trials of life are to be viewed in a new perspective. God seeks to use them to refine and deepen our trust, knowing that this process leads to maturity. Our response? Maintain steadfast confidence in Him.

32

James 1:5-8. Often pressures and uncertainty bring panic. We don't know which way to turn. We fear to make decisions, or we constantly change our minds. God is the kind of person who never reproaches us for limitations, but who, instead, promises us wisdom. But, James warns, a failure to keep looking to God will make it impossible for us to receive His guidance.

James 1:9-11. As individuals come into the family of God, all the old things which gave them their identity are denied, and a new identity is found. A poor man. once angry about his poverty, throws off the old attitude as he realizes that in his new relationship with God he has been raised to riches. A wealthy man, once confident in his status and pride, rejects both to praise God that through faith he has discovered his spiritual poverty. The old symbols of his pride are seen to be as perishable as grass.

James 1:12-15. Many circumstances may stimulate our desire to turn from God's way. James urges readers to realize that the root of temptation is not in the things that tempt us, but in ourselves. Candy may be a terrible temptation to a fat man on a diet, but another person who dislikes sweets won't even notice it. It is our inner reaction to the external stimulus that makes temptation. Recognizing this, we can clearly see that God's intention is never to cause us to fall. Instead, we are to learn that faith's life involves recognizing the roots of temptation within us and dealing with that first reaction by faith.

James 1:16-19. What can we expect from God?

Only "good" and "perfect" gifts. He never changes in His commitment to shower upon us His best. Through His good gifts, faith finds a way to victory over all that holds other men in a bondage which, without God, no man can break.

Faith's Interpersonal Impact (James 1:19–2:13). James then moves on to explore another dimension of faith's life. Men and women in relationship with Jesus find that faith not only touches them in the private aspects of their lives but also transforms their relationships with others.

James 1:19-21. The quick, hostile reactions of men to one another are changed by faith. Patience and meekness replace anger and pride.

James 1:22-25. At the heart of the believer's new way of living with others is the realization that God's Word is to be acted on, not just heard. The doer of God's Word is "blessed *in his doing*" (vs. 25).

James 1:26, 27. Faith's life-style is not demonstrated so much in "religious activity" as in compassion and justice. Pure and undefiled religion, James insists in an echo of the Old Testament prophets, is "to visit orphans and widows in their affliction, and to keep oneself unstained from the world" (vs. 27).

James 2:1-7. The unity found in Christ has its source in the fact that in His Church men *are* brothers. Rich and poor stand side by side in Him. Thus, in the Church, believers are to reject all artificial distinctions and to affirm unity in every way. Rich and poor are to be treated with equal respect and appreciation as persons; anything else is to blaspheme the Name by which we are called.

James 2:8-13. As men of faith, responsive to the royal law (the law of love set down by King Jesus), believers are to love their neighbors without partiality. Making distinctions within the brotherhood is as much transgression of the divine intent as other more obvious sins.

Believers, who are themselves "judged by the law that gives freedom" (vs. 12), are to be particularly sensitive to the way they live with others. In Christ, the old Law of restrictions has been replaced by a new law, a law that for the first time brings us freedom to live God's way. Through faith all that once was only held as an ideal is to become real.

GOING DEEPER
to personalize

1. Acts 4 describes the warm supportive relationship that began to develop in the new church. From that passage, list what you believe are marks of that relationship.

2. Which of the indications of *homothumadon* in Acts 4 seem most important to you personally? Which do you feel is most important for you to experience in your fellowship with other Christians?

3. Has there ever been a time when you felt something like Frank? What happened to you in that situation? Where did you find support?

4. James 1:1—2:13 contains advice and exhortation to those in the early church seeking to live faith's life. Using the outline beginning on page 32, select

35

one short section and examine it in depth. (1) Write out a paraphrase, expressing its thoughts in your own words. (2) In view of what you know from Acts about the early church, list several things James may have been thinking of when he wrote that section. (3) Illustrate the meaning of the section for today by outlining a "case history" (like that of Frank) to which the section and its guidelines might be applied.

to probe

1. What can you find out about the Book of James and its author? Explore in at least three commentaries or other sources.

2. Before looking at the next chapter of this text, read through James two or three times, and do an outline of the book. (That is, divide it into units of thought, marking the large ones by Roman numerals such as I, II, and III, and the shorter sections within each by 1, 2, 3, etc.)

BY FAITH

ONE OF THE STRIKING FEATURES of the Book of James is its frequent references to faith. In spite of this, though, James has not always been well received. Martin Luther, that great advocate of faith from the time of the Protestant Reformation, looked on James with suspicion and called it an "epistle of straw," certainly not a letter with the weight or importance of his favorites, Galatians and Romans.

Why did Luther hold such a dim view of the Book of James? The reason is not hard to find once we set his position against the backdrop of his cultural context and personal religious odyssey.

In Luther's day, the church was enduring one of its periodic cycles of corruption where the pattern of Biblical truth is perverted. A playboy pope, Leo X of the house of Medici, had succeeded to the papal chair and was selling the offices of the church to whoever could pay well for the privilege. The archbishop of Mainz, the primate of Germany, having borrowed the money to buy his office, was allowed to issue indulgences to recoup his expenses. These indulgences promised the complete and perfect remission of all sins to those (or their dead relatives or friends) who subscribed to the building of Saint Peter's Cathedral in Rome (though only one half of the money went for this purpose, the rest repaying the archbishop's loan). A popular jingle of the time phrased the promise well:

> As soon as the coin in the coffer rings,
> The soul from purgatory springs.

Luther had recently discovered for himself the tremendous truth that salvation, a person's entrance into a personal relationship with God, is a free gift received through faith in Jesus Christ. He realized that the Gospel, then, consists of what God, in Christ, has done for man. Man could never buy salvation!

Thus Luther and the other Reformers were drawn to those books of the Bible which stress the meaning of Christ's cross for all those who trust Him. James, with its ethical and practical emphasis on man's response to God's initiative, found little favor. In their situation it seemed at times to support the other side.

INTERPRETING SCRIPTURE

Luther's suspicion and others' misunderstanding of the Book of James point out an important feature of good Bible study and interpretation. *We must be care-*

ful to read Scripture in the context of its own time–not of our time.

Viewed from the perspective of the Protestant Reformation, James even seemed to contradict what is taught in the books of Galatians and Romans. All of James's talk of being "justified by works" seemed to deny Paul's affirmation that justification is by faith alone. With salvation viewed as the *entrance into* a relationship with God, James's approach (in which salvation is viewed as the continual outworking of the meaning of Christ's presence in the believer's life) is easy to misunderstand. Today, too, if we approach the New Testament with neat definitions of Bible terms fixed in our minds, remaining unaware of possible other meanings, we are liable to misunderstand some of the interplay of the great truths of God's Word.

One of the best ways to avoid misunderstanding the Bible, then, is to take a look at the circumstances in which a book was written. Then we go on to define the author's purpose. An important corollary is to look at the range of possible meanings of each significant Bible term and then decide which, in the context of the author's purpose and time, is intended.

We will want to keep the following two principles of interpretation in mind as we read the rest of the Book of James: (1) Understand the setting, and (2) look at all the possible meanings of terms. These two principles will help us discover not only the meaning of James but also the meaning of many other passages of God's Word.

The setting. What, then, was the setting in which James wrote? What was his purpose? And how do these differ from the setting of a book such as Galatians?

James wrote to the earliest church. He wrote in the days when the church was Hebrew-Christian, made up of men and women who had known the God of the Old Testament and who, under the dynamic preaching of the apostles, now recognized Jesus of Nazareth as their resurrected Lord and Savior. The Book of James is *not* an evangelistic book written to people in a culture where faith is foreign. The Book of James is a book of guidelines for living which was written to the family, to that early living community of believers who, with the full knowledge of who Jesus is, had chosen to make Him the center of their lives.

Essentially, then, James is concerned with how the new faith in Jesus is to find expression in the lives of members of that early *homothumadon* community. James is not a theological treatise or an attack on Paul's exposition of "faith alone." The two men are, in fact, exploring different aspects of a common salvation. Paul the obstetrician is explaining what happens at birth, and James the practical nurse is changing diapers and holding the hands of toddlers as they learn to walk. Because the setting and purpose of the two differ, a difference in emphasis naturally follows. As John Calvin pointed out in Luther's day, "It is not required that all handle the same arguments."

It's helpful to note several contrasts between the

setting of James and the setting and purpose of Paul's later letters.

JAMES	PAUL
stresses *the work of the believer* in relation to faith	stresses *the work of Christ* in relation to faith
is concerned that the *outcome of faith* be fruit (2:10), so that no one be permitted to confuse creeds with Christianity	is concerned that the *object of faith* be Christ, unmixed with self-reliance or self-righteousness
writes shortly after the Resurrection, when the Church is still Jewish, and the Old Testament well known	writes later, when the conversion of Gentiles has raised questions never asked or thought of earlier

These are important contrasts which help us see that we must understand James in James' own terms, not in terms of later developments in the early church or church history.

Key terms. We've already noted that *faith* is a common and key term in the Book of James, and we've indicated that faith has more than one impact in the believer's life. It is by faith that we enter into relationship with God. But it is also by faith that we continue to live our lives (see Rom. 1:17 and Hab. 2:4). What we must avoid when we read the Bible, then, is reading either the "saving" or the "life-style" meaning of faith into a particular verse until we have considered which meaning is intended *by the author*. Studying God's Word demands that we read to dis-

41

cover the writer's meaning, not to read our own impressions and theological presuppositions into what the writer says.

Another word that is often read into rather than read occurs not only in James but also throughout the New Testament. It is *saved.* To many people, whenever this word is found, it is automatically read as though the passage deals with entrance into a personal relationship with God. With some passages this creates no problem: "Everyone who calls on the name of the Lord will be saved" (Rom. 10:13), or "There is no other name under heaven given to men by which we must be saved" (Acts 4:12). Clearly these verses are dealing with that invitation to enter into eternal life through faith in Jesus.

But some other passages trouble those who have only a narrow view of the meaning of *saved.* James asks in chapter 2, "Can such faith save . . . ?" (vs. 14) and seems to answer that human works are somehow necessary. Is he denying Paul's teaching of salvation by grace through faith, apart from works (Eph. 2:8, 9)?

Paul himself writes in Philippians 2:12, "Continue to work out your salvation with fear and trembling." Is Paul contradicting here what he has written elsewhere? Is the Bible inconsistent? Is its teaching about salvation unclear?

The answer comes when we go back into the Old Testament and note that the root meaning of *salvation* is deliverance. In most cases the deliverance the Old Testament speaks of is from present dangers and tribulations. Only infrequently does salvation in the Old Testament context look beyond this life to focus on an individual's eternal destiny. The underlying theme is that God is a real person who does intervene in human affairs on behalf of those who trust Him.

In the New Testament it is more clearly defined just how God intervenes. Strikingly, God's intervention is pictured as something with past, present, and future implications. In the past, God acted in Jesus Christ to provide us with forgiveness of sins and a new life. By a simple act of faith we enter into all that Christ has done for us in history, and at that point in time we "are saved."

But God's intervention for us is not finished yet! In the person of the Holy Spirit, Jesus Himself has come into our lives. He has linked us to Himself with an unbreakable commitment; and because He is present in us, we are also "being saved." This is clearly what Paul is speaking of in Philippians: "Work out your salvation with fear and trembling," he writes, "for it is God who works in you to will and do what pleases him" (2:12, 13). We approach life seriously, but with confidence. Christ's *present-tense deliverance* is being worked out in our lives even as we continue to trust and rely on Him and as we demonstrate that trust by meeting life boldly, head on.

There is a future dimension of salvation as well. The Bible tells us that Jesus will return, and then we will be *fully* saved, fully delivered from all that sin has done to twist our personalities and warp us away from God (see Rom. 8:18-24).

It is important, then, when we come upon the

word *saved* in the Bible not to impose a single or narrow meaning on the word unthinkingly. What salvation is being spoken of here? Past tense? Present tense? Future? If we make this simple distinction and realize that each aspect of salvation affirms God as one who commits Himself to act in the lives of those who trust Him, we're freed both from misinterpreting the Bible and from many an agonizing doubt about our own personal standing with God.

Have you trusted in Christ and seen Him, the Nazarene who lived and died and rose again to bring you forgiveness of sin as your personal Savior? Then rejoice, and reach out to experience each dimension of all that that salvation means, without further doubts or fears.

JAMES

Let's return, then, to the Book of James, and look at it as God's guidance concerning *present-tense* salvation. Let's see how in its beginning the Church viewed faith's life-style.

Practicing faith. We looked in the previous chapter at James 1:2—2:13. There we saw James point out that faith touches every dimension of a person's life. Character (1:2-4), attitude (1:5-8), values (1:9-11), perceptions (1:12-18), emotional responses (1:19-21), behavior (1:22-27), and priorities (2:1-13) are all affected by faith. Entrance into the community of those who take Jesus as the focus of their lives brings a total reorientation of the individual and of all that he is. Christian faith is not merely assent to a set of

44

JAMES

Faith's Life-style

propositions about Jesus; it is in addition a whole new way of life!

Principles. James now goes on to state clearly and unequivocally the truth he has just demonstrated. He takes as an example an individual who claims to have faith, but whose "faith" seems unrelated to any expression of a faith life-style. "Can such faith save him?" (Jas. 2:14). "Such faith," the unresponse to the needs of brothers and sisters (and thus dramatically out of step with what the early church was experiencing as reported in Acts 4), is labeled by James as a dead faith. James goes on to point out that even the demons realize that there is one God. But their knowledge does not bring them into a relationship with God. It only brings them fear. Whatever saving faith may be, it can never be confused with mere intellectual assent.

45

No, true faith—trust in God rather than mere belief about Him—involves a dynamic relationship with a living person, which produces fruit. "Was not our ancestor Abraham considered righteous by what he did . . ." James (2:21) asks. "You see that his faith and his actions were working together, and his faith was made complete by what he did. And the scripture was fulfilled that says, 'Abraham believed God, and it was credited to him as righteousness' " (2:22, 23). Where there is true faith in God, that faith will not exist apart from works (vs. 26) but will instead find expression in the believer's life-style.

And so James calls us today to look at our Christian faith not only as *what* we believe, but also as *how* we believe. Has our response to God been a dry, intellectual kind of thing? Have we simply accepted as true the historical facts about Jesus' life and death and resurrection? Or have we gone beyond recognition to a wholehearted trust in Jesus? A trust that involves not only the confidence that He has forgiven us, but also the commitment of our whole person into His loving hands? A commitment of all that we have and are to Jesus now? A joyful acceptance of His invitation to fill our lives, as He did the men and women of the early church, with the Holy Spirit and with power?

Problems for faith. After his sweeping assertion of the principle that faith encompasses our life-style as well as our belief, James confronts us with problems that must be dealt with by that faith.

What is so surprising is that these are such common, ordinary problems! There is no demand here that our faith move mountains, produce miracles, or at the very least lead us to venture overseas without support to carry the Gospel to distant tribes. Rather than the extraordinary feats we sometimes associate with great faith, James directs our attention to the unspectacular business of the common man's daily life.

James 3:1-12. The tongue is a challenge for faith. It's easy for us to slip and criticize or cut our brother. The person who has his tongue under control has definitely matured in the life of faith (3:2).

James 3:13–4:10. Our own natural drives and desires are another challenge for faith. God's wisdom, which comes to us by faith (compare 3:17 with 1:5, 6), masters selfish motives and is marked by purity, peace, gentleness, reasonableness, mercy, and sincerity. Interpersonal conflict, whether between parents and children, husbands and wives, within the church, or internationally, comes from the passions (literally, "desires") that we permit to control us.

The person who has gained self-control and whose personality bears the marks of God's wisdom is someone who has grown much in the life of faith.

James 4:11, 12. Another common problem is our tendency to judge and evaluate each other with a view to condemning. God alone, who makes the law, is competent to judge. Faith struggles against this tendency to judge and criticize a neighbor.

James 4:13-17. Finally, faith comes into direct confrontation with pride. Arrogance, boasting, and approaching life as though everything were in our control rather than in God's hands is likely to grow

47

with age and accomplishments. Faith maintains the awareness that we are each dependent on God, and it frees us to relax in the assurance of His loving guidance for our lives.

Prospects and promises (Jas. 5:1-19). The men and women to whom James wrote lived, as we do, in a time when injustice was common and suffering the all too common lot of the believer and unbeliever alike. What does a life of faith promise to Jesus' follower? What are the rewards of joining others on faith's great adventure?

James 5:1-6. James wants us to recognize immediately that there is no promise of a utopia for us now. Instead James speaks for the oppressed, warning the wealthy who defraud the poor who labor for them while they live "in luxury and in pleasure" (vs. 5). Their treasures will rust away, all value lost, and the very rust will be evidence against them in the coming judgment.

The impact of this message is not to call the poor believer to vindictive joy at the prospect. Instead, it is to call rich and poor alike to the realization that a last day *is* coming when God will demonstrate His justice as well as His love to everyone. To the rich this message is a call to repentance; to the poor it is a message of hope. This world is not the sum and substance of reality. When Jesus comes, the world as well as individuals will be renewed.

James 5:7-20. And in the meantime? What resources does the man of faith have to draw on in this present world?

Many resources.

There is patience. Job waited, trusting God's timing. The end of Job's life proves the compassion and the mercy of God (Job 42). Like Job, the suffering believer today can steadfastly commit himself and his suffering to the Lord.

There is prayer. There is the privilege of joining with our brothers to bring both illness and sin to God for healing. And James insists that we should not underestimate the importance of prayer. "The prayer of a righteous man is powerful and effective" (5:16).

There is caring. This last resource is seen in the final words of James: "My brothers, if one of you should wander from the truth . . . " (5:19). The response of the community is not to condemn but to seek to restore. The community of faith is a community of love. Whatever life may hold outside the bonds of *homothumadon,* within the family there is the certainty of caring and concern.

In these last words, our attention is again turned to the picture of the early church which we saw sketched in Acts. In the context of God's new community, the challenge of faith's life-style is transformed. We are not alone. We go adventuring *with others!* In the company of brothers and sisters we find the acceptance, the love and the affirmation of our worth for which we all long.

GOING DEEPER
Let this chapter's introduction to James launch you into the study of the Bible text. Choose one or more of the following study projects.

to probe and personalize

1. On pages 42-44, the author mentioned different meanings of the word *saved*. Which meaning do you think is in view in each of the following?

Matthew 1:21 Hebrews 5:7 Acts 2:21
Luke 7:50 Hebrews 7:25 Romans 5:10
I Timothy 1:15 Isaiah 30:15 Ephesians 2:8

2. The author notes that James 1:2—2:13 touches on many dimensions of human life, including values, attitudes, behavior, etc. (p. 44). For each, find at least one illustration of how faith might touch that aspect of our lives in addition to the one James gives.

3. James 2:14-26 is a much misunderstood passage, largely because of the tendency to read into such words as *justified* a preconceived theological meaning. Rewrite this passage in your own words (paraphrase) to express what you feel James intends.

4. Select one of the four problem areas found in 3:1—4:17. Study it carefully, and do the following:

   a), Carefully study the section you choose. Make sure you understand the reasoning of James.

   b), Write a brief description of a modern situation to which James' teaching applies.

   c), Explain how the teaching of James gives guidance to the individuals in your situation.

   d), Jot down how this teaching applies to your own life and present experience.

5. Compare James 5:7-19 with Acts 2—4. How does the description of the early church in Acts help us understand more fully the implications of James 5?

REACH OUT

"WHAT'S HAPPENED TO US? We were so close before. And then we started growing . . . and . . . ." Carol's words reflect a common experience. A little group of believers comes together, grows close, and forms a local church. There's an exciting sense of closeness and warmth and enthusiasm.

As time passes, growth comes. We become busier and busier. New people come in whom we don't know, and before long the closeness we felt with earlier friends is lost. Soon decisions about buildings and parking lots and programs and staffing and so many other things crowd in on us.

It's easy then to look back at the earlier days and to long for the intimacy of that smaller group. It's also easy, if we've never experienced that kind of fellowship, to doubt whether it is even possible in this day and age.

All such longing is not only useless; it is also foolish. It is in the very nature of life to reproduce. It is in the very nature of Christian faith and life to reach out, to welcome more and more people into the family of God. It may be more difficult to maintain warmth and a sense of oneness in a church when growth comes. But the solution is never to push back to the past. The solution is in finding new ways to affirm and to experience our *homothumadon*.

It was no different in the early church. With growth and expansion came tensions. There were disagreements. There was sin. There were suspicion and misunderstanding. But through it all the early church expected that God the Holy Spirit would enable them to experience the unity that He Himself had fashioned in that bond which knits believers to Jesus and to one another.

GROWING TENSION
Acts 5–7

These three chapters of Acts bring us back again to look at the Jerusalem church. There, with growth, came tensions from both within the believing community and from without.

Sin (Acts 5:1-11). The first tension emerged from within. A couple named Ananias and Sapphira wanted a reputation for benevolence, like that of other believers who had sold their possessions for the benefit of the whole church. But Ananias and Sapphira didn't want to give all.

There was no demand by God or the believing community that they should give all. As Peter asked, "After it was sold, wasn't the money at your disposal?" (5:4). But rather than openly giving a part, the two conspired to pretend that they had turned the full purchase price over to the church.

The sin was not in the choice they made of the use of their possessions; the sin was in their hypocrisy and in the lie they attempted to tell not only to the brotherhood but also to the Holy Spirit.

God's judgment was swift. Both died. And the whole church **was** gripped with a deep sense of reverence and awe for God (called "fear" in the text).

Here is a remedy for our insensitivity as well. Let's regain awareness of just who this God is who has called us into a relationship with Himself. When we are filled with awe because *God* is present with us, the little pretenses and games we play with one another are quickly set aside.

Official persecution (Acts 5:12-42). The aggressive preaching of the apostles, authenticated by "signs and wonders" (healing miracles), led to a revival. "More and more men and women," the Bible says, "believed in the Lord" (vs. 14). This success filled the religious leaders with jealousy; they angrily imprisoned the apostles. But Peter and the others were released by an angel. By daybreak they were again speaking "the full message of this Life" (vs. 20) to eager crowds.

The Temple guards were ordered to rearrest the apostles. Afraid of the people's reaction, the guards "invited" the apostles to come with them rather than attempting to drag them away. The Jewish leaders were furious at the disciples' continued charge that the Jesus they themselves had killed was now exalted by God to be Savior and Lord. The leaders now wanted to murder the Twelve as well! Instead, they commanded the apostles not to tell others about Jesus and let them go.

The response of the Twelve sets the pattern for our response to similar pressures. "Day after day, in the temple courts and from house to house, they never stopped teaching and proclaiming the good news that Jesus is the Christ" (vs. 42).

Suspicion within (Acts 6:1-7). As the number of disciples continued to increase, some of the Greek-speaking Jewish believers felt that their widows were being neglected when the resources of the church were distributed. This group of believers was made up of foreign-born Jews who had gathered for Pentecost from several different lands (see Acts 2:8-10). They first heard the apostles' message in their own languages. Later, not knowing the Aramaic language of Palestine, they could communicate in Greek, the common second language of the Roman world.

Suspicious of the motives of the native-born stewards in charge of the distribution, these Hellenists raised a complaint that might have hardened into a bitter split if it had not been handled wisely.

What happened was that the apostles called the church together and told them to "choose seven men from among you who are known to be full of the Spirit and wisdom" (6:3). These would be responsible for the distribution. The men they chose had names like Stephen and Philip, which identify

54

them as Hellenists. The misunderstanding was healed. "So the word of God spread. The number of disciples in Jerusalem increased rapidly" (6:7).

The corporate witness of the church to the reality of Jesus' presence in their community brought its own sure response (see Jn. 13:34).

Hatred (Acts 6:8–7:59). The success of the church, and particularly its constant affirmation of Jesus, now brought a strong reaction. The preaching of the Gospel had polarized Jerusalem. Some responded to the message, while many others became just as hardened opponents of the church as they had been of Jesus during His earthly life.

The growing anger now broke out in a vicious mob attack on Stephen. Stephen's defense before the mob (Acts 7) traced the spiritual hardness of Israel from the days of Moses to the present. It was a bold challenge to these men, in which they were charged with faithlessness to the God they claimed to serve. Enraged, the listening crowd dragged Stephen outside the city gates and battered his body with stones until he died.

Thus the church offered up the blood of her first martyr, who prayed for his murderers as he died, "Lord, do not hold this sin against them" (7:60).

EXPANSION
Acts 8

Christ in His final charge to His disciples had told them to wait in Jerusalem until the Holy Spirit came to bring them power. Then they were to reach out beyond Jerusalem to share Jesus with the entire world. In Acts 1:8 Jesus gave a pattern for that expansion: "You will be my witnesses in Jerusalem, and in all Judea and Samaria, and to the ends of the earth."

This pattern, in fact, gives us a way to outline the Book of Acts and also a framework in which to place the New Testament letters written during the early decades of the Church.

There are several ways to outline the Acts' history of the early church. One is to see this record as a report first of Peter's ministry to the Jews (Acts 1—12), followed by a report of Paul's mission to the Gentile world (Acts 13—28). Another is to see it as a history of the development of the Christian movement: its origins (1—5), its transition days (5—12), and its expansion to become a world religion (13—28). However, perhaps the best way to see it is in the framework of Acts 1:8, as the record of an expanding, dynamic life-force, reaching out to bring more and more of mankind into a vital relationship with Jesus Christ.

Judea and Samaria. The death of Stephen launched a great persecution against the church in Jerusalem. The believers, except for the apostles, were driven out and scattered throughout Judea and Jerusalem.

Everywhere the believers went they told others about Christ, and the message was received—even in Samaria.

The response of the Samaritans must have been something of a surprise. While the people of this

NEW TESTAMENT TIMES

A.D.*	Predominant Personality in Acts	Writings
35	Peter	
40		
45		
50	James	James, Galatians
55	Paul	Mark, 1 & 2 Thess.
60		1 & 2 Cor., Rom., Luke
65		Matt., Eph., Col., Philem. Phil., 1 Peter, Acts
70		Jude, 1 & 2 Tim., Titus 2 Peter, Hebrews
75		
80		
85		
90		
95		John, 1, 2, & 3 John
100		Revelation

* Not all scholars accept this dating system. For example, Galatians is sometimes dated after I Thessalonians. The arguments pro and con are quite complex, however, and it is not in the best interests of the survey approach to present these details. It would be good, though, to familiarize oneself with the basic points of the arguments, and this can be done by referring to any good book of New Testament introduction.

57

district were viewed as mongrel Jews until excom-
municated by Judaism in about A.D. 300, they were
looked down on as a semiheretical and "foolish" sect.

The origin of the Samaritans goes back to the
deportation of the people of the northern kingdom
of Israel in 722 B.C. Those Jews still left in the land
mingled with other people imported by Assyria to
form a loose culture that retained much of the Old
Testament tradition but developed its own theology
and worship system. That the Samaritans had seriously distorted the revealed faith is clear from Jesus'
conversation with a Samaritan woman, recorded in
John 4, and also from Jesus' clear distinction between Israel and Samaria during His days on earth
(see Mt. 10: 5-7).

Now, however, the Samaritans not only heard the
Gospel, but "the multitudes with one accord gave
heed" (Acts 8: 6, KJV). Hearing reports of the mass
conversion, the apostles sent Peter and John to investigate. Discovering that these men and women
had truly believed, Peter prayed for them that they
might also be given the gift of the Holy Spirit.

This significant incident in the life of the early
church receives varying interpretations. What is important to observe here, however, is that the pro-
gression of the church outward from Jerusalem
(Acts 1: 8) proceeded in a series of steps that were
given the seal of approval of God's Spirit. Here the
Samaritans, later the Gentiles (Acts 10: 44-46;
19: 1-6).

Since the 700-year-old antagonism between
Samaritan and Jew had some of its roots in religious

rivalry, it would have been so easy for the Samaritans to accept the new faith but continue to affirm their identity as a group separate from Christian Jews. By mediating the gift of the Spirit through Peter, God not only affirmed the unity of the Church as a single community but also affirmed the authority of the apostles whom Jesus had chosen to lead it during the early years.

Simon Magus. Acts 8 tells us that Peter's act in Samaria was misunderstood by at least one observer. Simon, a magician who had won a large following among the Samaritans, offered the apostles money if they would only give him such power.

THE PROGRESSION OF THE CHURCH

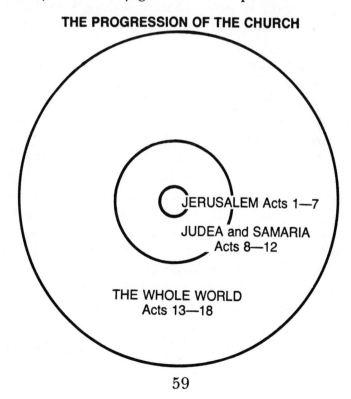

JERUSALEM Acts 1—7

JUDEA and SAMARIA
Acts 8—12

THE WHOLE WORLD
Acts 13—18

Magicians were well known in the ancient world and are spoken of in both Old and New Testaments. Our word is derived, through the Latin and ancient Greek, from *Magi,* a priestly clan in Persia. From the first century A.D. on, the word was used of a variety of magicians, soothsayers, and astrologers. The usual guiding motive behind the life of such a person was the acquisition of power to influence people and events through occult knowledge and arcane practice.

The Scripture makes it clear that this stands in direct conflict with God and His ways (see Deut. 18:10-14; Gal. 5:19). There *are* supernatural powers under the control of Satan; seeking knowledge or power through the occult and spirit world is unquestionably anti-God.

Acts 8 records Peter's stern rebuke of Simon. We hear nothing more of this magician in the Biblical record. There is, however, early tradition of a heretical sect from the same era called the Simoniani. Whether or not this sect sprang from this Simon whom Peter confronted has never been confirmed.

The chapter closes with the report of the conversion of an Ethiopian government official. He was apparently a convert to Judaism, or at least a "Godfearer" who believed in Israel's God but had not undergone the rites of conversion. The Holy Spirit led Philip away from Samaria and brought him to explain to the Ethiopian eunuch the way of salvation as expressed in the Old Testament passage of Isaiah 53.

Hebrew believers had begun to fan out across the

ancient world. The Gospel message was carried with them. This seed would soon bring a rich harvest.

GENTILE CONVERTS
Acts 10, 11

Chapter 9 of Acts tells of the conversion of Paul, an event we'll examine in the next chapter. And then the Acts history sketches one of the least expected events in the Bible.

Gentile believers suddenly are welcomed into the Church with the same rights and privileges and blessings as the Jewish believers! And again at this turning point, the central figure is the apostle Peter.

Peter. Peter and his brother Andrew were both members of the original Twelve. They were fishermen, perhaps in partnership with and certainly friends of James and John.

The Gospels show that Peter was leader of the Twelve. He is listed first in the four New Testament lists of the disciples. He is the most frequently mentioned disciple. With James and John, Peter was a member of the inner circle of Jesus' intimates. In Acts Peter clearly has had the leading role, from his preaching of the first sermon on Pentecost, to mediating the Spirit to the Samaritans, and now to first proclaiming the Gospel to Gentiles.

While a leader, Peter remains a man of contrasts. He was bold, yet unstable. Quick to recognize Jesus as God's Christ, Peter was just as quick to object when Jesus spoke of the coming cross (Mt. 16). Ready to promise commitment to the death, Peter three times denied the Lord on the night of His trial (Mk. 14).

In Acts the inconsistent Peter of the Gospels seems to have emerged as a man of firm and consistent leadership. Yet, later at Antioch, Peter would refuse to eat with Gentile converts for fear of the criticism of his Hebrew-Christian companions.

Peter stands as a reminder to us to rely on the stabilizing and strengthening power of the Holy Spirit. God can take our strengths and natural gifts and use them, and He alone can protect us from our weaknesses. Because the Spirit *is* with us, we too can expect to live victoriously.

After these chapters, the focus of Acts shifts to the apostle Paul. Tradition tells us that Peter continued his ministry among the Jewish people and traveled widely. Two of his last letters are found in the New Testament, the last being written shortly before his own martyrdom. Early historians seem to agree that Peter died in Rome, executed during the violent persecution of Christians by the emperor Nero in A.D. 64.

The centurion (Acts 10, 11). In the Gentile center of Caesarea, an officer of the Roman army who had come to believe in God was visited by an angel. The angel told the officer, Cornelius, to summon Peter, who would communicate God's message to him.

The next day, as the Roman's messengers were on the way to Joppa where Peter was staying, Peter had a vision. Three times a sheet filled with animals forbidden by Jewish law as food (this is the meaning of "unclean" here) was lowered from heaven. Three times a voice commanded Peter to eat. And three times Peter protested against the divine command. Each time the lesson was driven home: "Do not call anything impure that God has made clean" (Acts 10:15).

While Peter was puzzling about the meaning of the vision, Cornelius's messengers knocked at the door.

Gentiles. To understand the need for Peter's preparation and the angry reaction of the believers when they heard later that Peter had actually gone into a Gentile's home, we need to realize the attitude of the Jew toward all foreigners.

For hundreds of years the Jews, full of a sense of their own destiny as God's chosen people, had been politically subject to a series of foreign rulers. Vicious wars, filled with unspeakable atrocities, had been waged by and against the foreigners. Yet, the Jews remained in bondage. The fact that this bondage was to men who had no standing or covenant relationship with God made the situation even more galling. Israel was forced to submit to a race they considered unholy and with whom they would never choose to associate. The Gentile was viewed with far greater loathing and with less respect than the slave of colonial days. In fact, no pious Jew would ever enter a Gentile's home. He would be contaminated if he did, unable to worship God until he had been ceremonially cleansed.

Thus in the earliest days of the Church the believers were astounded to find God extending His Spirit to the Gentiles. This called for a radical reorientation of their conception of God and of themselves as the chosen people.

At Cornelius' home. Peter, taught by the vision of the unclean animals lowered from heaven, went with Cornelius' messengers. He entered the centurion's home and began to speak: "You are well aware that it is against our law for a Jew to associate with a Gentile or visit him. But God has shown me that I should not call any man impure or unclean" (10:28). Peter had responded quickly to God; he accepted a concept that, nevertheless, would keep on dividing the Church for generations!

Cornelius told of the angel's visit. Now he and his family and friends were eager to hear what God would tell them through Peter.

So Peter began to speak about Jesus. He repeated again the basic apostolic Gospel we've seen in Acts 2 and 3 and again in chapter 4. And as Peter was speaking, the Holy Spirit fell on all who heard.

The Jewish contingent with Peter was amazed. They heard these Gentiles speaking in tongues just as they themselves had at Pentecost. It was clear that God had given these Gentiles the same gift that He had given them. Recognizing that God had revealed His will, Peter had the whole Gentile company baptized in the name of Jesus Christ.

Chapter 11 reports the reaction of some in the Jerusalem church. They attacked Peter sharply. Peter went over the events step by step and shared this unanswerable conclusion: "So if God gave them the same gift as he gave us when we believed in the Lord Jesus Christ, who was I to think that I could oppose God!" (vs. 17). And the passage reports, "They had no further objections and praised God saying, 'So, then, God has even granted the Gentiles repentance unto life.' " (vs. 18).

A new and exciting day had come for the early church. Soon the whole world would be invited to go adventuring.

GOING DEEPER
to personalize

1. Read through Acts 5—11 twice; the first time quickly, the second time more slowly, underlining thoughts and phrases that seem significant to you.

2. In a single sentence express what you believe God is saying to us today in each of the four stories of tension in the early church (Acts 4—7; text pp. 52-55).

3. Considering their cultural viewpoint, the response of the majority in the early church to Gentile conversion was an amazing phenomenon and clear evidence of the reality of God's presence in their lives.

What parallels are there in our own society and culture? What groups are alienated from one another? What are the implications of the Gospel for such divisions? How do you think Christ's presence in His Church today is (or might be) shown in this area?

to probe

1. Research more completely the attitude of the Jews of Jesus' day toward Gentiles.

ON MISSION

THE PENNSYLVANIA CHURCH was angry now.

Their young pastor had reached out to the bearded youths, spillovers of the West Coast hippie movement of the late sixties. And he had seen God touch a number of them. At first everyone had been delighted; God accepted these dropouts of society as well as respectable people like themselves!

But then the conflict began. The young people didn't appreciate the church music; they grooved on guitars. The formal, sixty-minute service of the church seemed like empty ritual to the youth; they wanted to sit around for hours and talk. And the appearance of beards and blue jeans on Sunday morning—in church!—seemed more than a little sacrilegious to the middle-class church members.

When I visited the church, a compromise of sorts had been worked out. The young people wouldn't come to the church services. But they did have their own services later Sunday evening—in the church basement.

There had been honest joy in the church at the realization that the message of Jesus could reach these outcasts. But going on to work out the nature of the relationship between the two cultural groups was difficult indeed.

This Pennsylvania church was experiencing something that all of us face in different ways and with different intensity: the problem of the "open church." In the community of faith, can we accept those of different cultural or racial background? Can we welcome them, invite them to become one with us, and value their differences? Can we see in those differences a gift that God has given to enrich us? Or will we let our differences cut us off from our brothers? Or, worse still, will we demand that our brothers adopt our own culture and ways as the price of belonging?

As the number of Gentiles in the early church grew, and as some local congregations developed that were predominantly Gentile, this was an issue the apostles and elders were forced to face. How *are* we to relate to those who are significantly "different"?

PERSECUTION INTENSIFIES
Acts 11:19–12:25

Outbreaks of persecution in Palestine continued. The believers were scattered beyond Judea and

67

Samaria. They spread along the Mediterranean coast and crossed the waters to Cyprus. At first these Hebrew Christians shared Jesus only within the Jewish communities. But then some began to speak of Jesus to Gentiles as well. And, at Antioch (see map, p. 70), a great number of Gentiles believed and turned to the Lord!

The Jerusalem church again sent an investigating committee, headed by Barnabas, a man we first met in Acts 4: 36, 37. Barnabas was delighted by what he found. He encouraged and taught the Gentile converts, and then, led by the Holy Spirit, set out to find a man named Saul, who is known in history as Paul, apostle to the Gentiles and writer of the bulk of our New Testament Epistles.

Saul was probably then a man in his early forties. He had been a Pharisee, one of that strict sect of Jews from which had come Christ's most vigorous enemies. A few years before, Saul had been a witness to Stephen's martyrdom. He had become filled with hatred for this heretical sect of "the Way" and had become one of the foremost persecutors in Judea. As the "heresy" spread, Saul had applied to the high priest for a commission to go to the Syrian city of Damascus and bring any followers of Jesus back to Jerusalem in chains.

On the road to Damascus, Paul had been thrown to the ground as a brilliant light flashed from heaven, and Jesus Himself spoke to him. Blinded, Saul had stumbled into Damascus and waited in darkness until the Lord sent a member of the church there to restore his sight.

Converted through this unique confrontation, Saul had become an open and vigorous proponent of the faith he had earlier attacked. He'd been so bold that members of the Jewish community in Damascus had finally determined to kill him. Escaping, Saul had returned to Jerusalem and sought out the brotherhood. But no one would associate with him. They were afraid that it was a ruse to break into the Christian "underground."

Finally Barnabas had taken the risk. Convinced of Saul's sincerity, Barnabas had brought him to the apostles.

Saul had begun to boldly and publicly proclaim the new faith in Jerusalem. Again the Jews had determined to kill him. Finally Saul had been forced to flee from Jerusalem and was returned by the brothers to Tarsus. Then for a time the Judean church knew a relaxation of persecution.

Now Barnabas went to Tarsus to look for Paul. They returned together to Antioch, and the two became part of a leadership team that ministered to the believers there. Later, when the Holy Spirit warned of a famine coming in Judea, Barnabas and Saul were selected to take the funds collected by this Gentile church to their Jewish brethren.

In the meantime, persecution had again intensified in Palestine. This time it came from an official source (Acts 12). James, one of the Twelve, was executed by King Herod Agrippa, who ruled as a puppet and vassal of Rome. This so pleased the Jewish community that Herod had Peter arrested as well, intending to execute him at the conclusion of

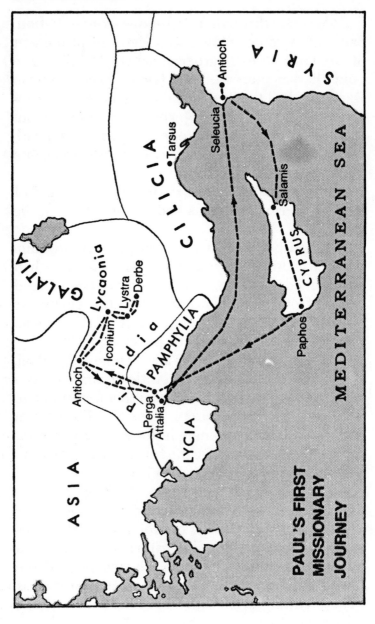

70

the Passover feast. Peter was miraculously released by an angel and went into hiding. Herod himself now bore the brunt of God's judgment; he was suddenly stricken with an extremely painful disease and died.

Persecution slacked again. Barnabas, with Saul and a young man named John Mark (who later would write the Gospel of Mark), returned to Antioch.

THE FIRST GENTILE MISSION
Acts 13, 14

Earlier, the witness to the Gentiles had been an unplanned overflow of witness by Hebrew Christians to other Jews. Now, for the first time God spoke to the Gentile church of Antioch, commanding that two men be set aside for a specific mission to Gentiles (compare 13:2 with 9:15). As the Holy Spirit directed, Barnabas and Saul (soon to be called Paul in the Acts text) were ordained for this mission.

Acts 13:4-12. At the first stop on the journey Barnabas and Paul began their mission by preaching in the synagogue to the Jews. Soon they were sharing the Gospel not only with Gentiles but with the Roman proconsul (governor). Here Paul, like Peter, had a confrontation with a magician, an apostate Jew named Bar-Jesus ("son of the deliverer"). The evil sorcerer was stricken with blindness; the Roman leader believed.

Acts 13:13-52. Traveling on, the missionary team went to the city of Antioch in the province of Pisidia. Again, as Paul always did, he went first to the Jews

71

and proclaimed Jesus in the synagogue. This pattern in missionary work remained consistent throughout his life. He continued to have a great love for his own people. He was convinced that they, the people through whom the Savior had been given to the world, must have the first opportunity to hear the Gospel. This approach also had other benefits. In every synagogue there was a place reserved for "God-fearers." These were Gentiles who had been drawn to the high moral precepts and exalted concept of a single, sovereign Creator God, which characterized Judaism alone of all the then current religions.

In Pisidian Antioch, many Jews and many of the devout Gentiles responded to the Gospel. As the sermon recorded in Acts 13:16-41 shows, Paul's message was the very same apostolic Gospel that had been preached by Peter some twelve or fifteen years earlier.

The response of the city was explosive. The next Sabbath "almost the whole city" (vs. 44) gathered to hear what the apostles had to say. Many of the Gentiles believed. The Jews, jealous and angry, stirred up the leaders of the city and drove the missionary team away.

Acts 14:1-7. Traveling to Iconium, the team launched a new mission, and the now-familiar pattern was repeated. Beginning to preach at the synagogue, they soon gathered a crowd of converts from both Jewish and Gentile populations. The unbelieving Jews reacted angrily and stirred up a Jewish and Gentile reaction. The population of the

EVENTS OF PAUL'S LIFE

A.D. 34	Conversion
A.D. 36	To Tarsus for "the silent years"
A.D. 46	To Antioch
A.D. 47-48	First missionary journey
A.D. 48	Jerusalem council
A.D. 49	Writes first Epistle (Galatians)
A.D. 50-51	Second missionary journey
A.D. 53	Third missionary journey begins
A.D. 59	Journey to Rome
A.D. 64	Martyrdom

city was divided. Finally the unbelieving majority physically attacked and drove out the missionaries.

Acts 14:8-23. At Lystra, a city with no significant Jewish population, the mission began in a very different way. The healing of a cripple was observed by crowds, and Paul and Barnabas were mistaken for gods come down to earth. By the time the missionaries grasped what was happening, the local priests were about to offer up an animal sacrifice to them!

Distraught, the missionaries rushed to explain that they were merely men. But, they *were* bearers of good news from the God who had made all things, and whose many gifts testified to His goodness. The people of the city listened.

But again a contingent of Jews from Antioch and Iconium arrived. These men had determined to follow the missionaries and try to undo their preaching, and they succeeded in arousing the city against

Paul. Paul was attacked with cobblestones, dragged out of the city, and left for dead.

But the "dead" Paul got up and returned to the city. The next day the missionary team began to retrace its steps, visiting again those groups of believers which had been formed in every place they had been.

Several patterns established on this first missionary trip to Gentile lands continued to mark the evangelism of Paul and of the other Christians throughout the days of the early church:

- They visited cities and lands where the Gospel had not been heard.
- They began their mission in the synagogues, first contacting the Jewish community and those Gentiles who had been drawn to Israel's God.
- The message quickly was shared with the whole city, and the response was quicker from the Gentiles than from the Jews.
- Initial successes led to persecution and opposition.
- After establishing the new group of believers by usually spending weeks or months with them to teach them, the missionary team moved on.
- Later the missionary team returned. Those who had grown spiritually and had been marked off for leadership by the Holy Spirit were recognized and ordained as local leaders by the apostles.
- The missionary team, and particularly Paul, remained in contact with the new church. Letters of teaching and encouragement were sent, and often men like Titus and Timothy were dispatched to teach and to help guide the new church for a time.

■ Each new church, however, was to depend on the leading and guidance of the Holy Spirit. As the independent congregation matured, that group of believers reached out to the nearby cities and towns to share the message of Jesus in their own local "Jerusalem and Judea."

The explosive, multiplying dynamic of the Church of Jesus Christ, infused with His Spirit and committed to live life's great adventure by focusing on its Lord, had begun the process by which the Roman world would be reached in a single generation.

THE ROMAN WORLD

The world into which the Church now went adventuring was very different from the provincial land of Palestine. Centuries earlier the conqueror, Alexander the Great, had begun a process which spread Greek culture and language across the Middle East. Asia Minor, Egypt, the Greek isles, and the ancient empire of Persia all fell to the conqueror and, after his early death, to the four generals who divided Alexander's spoils.

The spread of the Greek language and culture unified and linked the world of the New Testament. The vision of "one world" and of a "united nations" is no modern invention! It was Alexander's dream hundreds of years before Christ. By the days of the early church, this dream had been realized to the extent that missionaries like Barnabas and Paul did not have the language barrier that missionaries face today. They could communicate wherever they went in Greek, the second language of elite and commoner alike.

Greece conquered the world culturally. But it had taken the expansionist and brutal power of Rome to weld the world together politically. Under the first emperor, Augustus, the Pax Romana (Roman peace) had been imposed by force of arms. The empire which Rome held included not only Egypt and the Middle East but extended even to the British Isles, encompassing France, Spain, and what is now West Germany. Roman government and Roman law brought an unprecendented stability to the world through which the missionaries traveled. There was no trouble with passports, no detours for wars between bickering states. During the first years of Christianity's expansion, when it was still considered a sect of Judaism by the government, the Christian faith was an authorized religion, its freedom to practice guaranteed by the Roman government itself!

The Roman world was far less unified religiously than it was politically. The official religion of the empire was the cult of emperor worship. The classic religion of the period of the Roman Republic (with its worship of a pantheon of interchangeable Greek and Roman gods headed by Zeus or Jupiter) received only perfunctory attention. But existing alongside the official and the classic religions were a number of secret cults generally referred to as mystery religions. These originated in the East and became more and more popular as the aberrations of succeeding emperors eroded confidence in the official religion. The austere and distant gods of Greece and Rome offered no personal relationship and provided no personal religious experience. To fill this need, cults like the Eleusinian, the Dionyisian, the cult of the Great Mother (Cybele), and that of the Egyptian Isis and Osiris, spread through the empire.

These mystery religions featured initiation rituals, rites, and myths. The cults had little or no ethical content. Most stressed fertility in a female deity and had both a sexual and social appeal. In the sense of belonging that came through initiation into the cult, and in the promise of a special relationship with a mythical deity, many looked for a meaning that life in the Roman Empire, for all its stability, did not provide.

The world, empty of promise or hope, was ready for the coming of the Savior. And this world over which Rome ruled was uniquely shaped to permit the explosive spread of the one faith which actually did meet the deepest needs of man, a faith which rested not on myth but on the historical fact of God's entrance into the world in the person of His own Son, Jesus.

ACTS 15

The missionary team returned to Antioch filled with joy, eager to report what God had done among the Gentiles (14:24-28).

But soon another kind of team appeared. These were men who came from Judea, who had been thinking seriously about the relationship between the Jewish church and the growing number of Gentile congregations. Their solution was to go back to a principle that had operated in Old Testament times. If a person who was not born a Jew wished to become a worshiper of God, he must first convert to Judaism. Identification with the people of the Covenant was the one way to enter fully into relationship with the God of the Covenant.

And so they began to move into the Gentile churches, teaching that "unless you are circumcised according to the custom [the Law] taught by Moses, you cannot be saved" (15:1). To really be a Christian, they thought one had to first become a Jew or at least surrender one's own culture and identify fully with the culture and life-style of the Israelites.

This teaching stimulated a serious debate particularly when it became clear that these teachers had not been sent by the apostles and did not represent the official position of the Jerusalem congregation.

A delegation was sent from Antioch, led by Paul and Barnabas, to bring this issue to the apostles at Jerusalem. There, in about A.D. 49, the first council of the church was held.

Paul and Barnabas reported on the great moving of God among the Gentiles. Then they heard the demand made by some believers who were also Pharisees (the most strict of Judaism's sects when it came to stressing man's obligation to keep both the written Law of Moses and oral tradition): "The Gentiles must be circumcised and required to obey the law of Moses" (15:5).

The Law. In the next chapters of our study we'll discuss the Law in depth. For now, it's important to realize that the term is used in a number of ways, both in and out of Scripture.

At times *law* (*nomos* in Greek) is rendered "custom." At other times our word *principle* is more fitting. But even when *the law of Moses* is specified, there may be different referents. At times *the law* is used synonymously with *the first five books of Moses* (the Pentateuch). At other times it points specifically to the moral law expressed in the Ten Commandments. At other times *the law* may be a way of referring to revelation itself, meaning God's total revelation of Himself and His will in the Scriptures. Finally, *the law* spoke of the life-style of Israel, regulated as it was by Biblical commands and traditions that patterned the way the Jew spoke and thought and acted. The Pharisees certainly believed that *the law* spoke to that distinctive way of life which set them apart from all foreigners and marked them as God's peculiar people.

In Acts it seems clear that the challengers were asking for more than moral and ethical purity from the Gentile converts. "It is necessary," they insisted, "to circumcise them, and to charge them to keep the law of Moses" (15:5). Circumcision was the sign of entry into the Covenant relationship with God, the visible mark of being a Jew. The Pharisees were demanding that Gentile converts reject their own culture and heritage and adopt both the name and life-style of the Jew to be accepted as true Christians!

Acts 15 reports the struggle of the leaders with

this issue, and it reports the exciting outcome. The Law, Peter declared, was a burden no one had ever been able to bear successfully (15:10). Since salvation is by the grace of God for Jew and Gentile alike, why burden the Gentile believers with the Law?

After further discussion, James summed up the council's conclusion. God clearly has acted to save Gentiles *as Gentiles.* In fact, the Old Testament prophets foretold a time when such a thing would happen and even Gentiles would be called by His name (15:17). The Hebrew church had to, then, let the Gentiles keep on being Gentiles. They had to accept their brothers *as they were.*

There were also four specific warnings which related to aspects of the Gentile life-style which James felt should be brought to their special attention. These four warnings seem rooted in prohibitions that were stated by God before the Law was given (see Gen. 9). The Christian converts were to have nothing to do with the idol worship that characterized their culture. They were to keep away from illicit sex (again, a common feature of the Gentiles' life-style). They were to give up unbutchered meat (something tremendously offensive to the Jew, which would have made it very hard for a Jew to have fellowship with a Gentile brother; see Lev. 17:10-14; Deut. 12:16, 23, 25), and they were to abstain from shedding blood (this probably means cruelty, murder, and even possibly service in the army. Later Christians apparently did take it this way; many refused to do military service and were executed. Others did serve in the Roman army but were persecuted for their refusal to enter into the official religious practices expected of soldiers.)

The delegation returned joyfully to Antioch. The Jerusalem church had officially welcomed the Gentiles into the fellowship of the Christians. It had affirmed the fact that every culture has equal standing before God. From Jew and Gentile, God was about to form one new man. In Christ, the differences could be accepted and forgotten. Jesus, not our differences from one another, was to always be the focus of each life.

The problem would, of course, surface again and again. Paul, the leader of the Antioch delegation, would himself be the one to spell out in letters to the Galatians and Romans just what the Law does mean to a Christian. But those days were still ahead.

For now, another great stride had been made along the road of adventure. And the Church knew a special sense of joy and peace.

GOING DEEPER
to personalize

Read through Acts 11—15; then go back over it and explore the following:

1. Compare Paul's sermon in Acts 13 with Peter's in Acts 2 and 3.

2. In Acts 13 and 14, review the pattern of missionary effort (text, pp. 73, 74). How do you think this pattern is related to our evangelism today? Does it give us guidance for our approach to sharing Jesus? How?

3. Study Acts 15, guided by the discussion on pages 76-80 of the text. Then look again at the true story related to the beginning of the chapter (text, p. 66). What principles from Acts 15 apply to this case? How might those principles be applied? What steps might be taken by the two congregations to apply them? In two years, what would you expect the pattern of life at the Pennsylvania church to be like?

to probe
1. Research the situation in the Roman world as the Church began its missionary explosion. Or examine one of its following aspects:
   a. culture
   b. language
   c. political situation
   d. religions
2. *Before reading the next chapter of the text,* study the following passages and do a character sketch of the apostle Paul, concentrating on his personality, motives, relationships, etc.:

Acts 9
Galatians 1
Philippians 3
II Corinthians 1
I Thessalonians 2

Galatians 1, 2; Acts 9; Philippians 3
II Corinthians 1; I Thessalonians 2

"THE APOSTLE"

"HISTORY," SOMEONE ONCE SAID, "is biography." What he meant, of course, is that we cannot understand the past without understanding the great men who appear at crucial times to lead nations or movements or mankind itself into new eras.

Throughout the Bible we are confronted with great men. Abraham. Moses. Joshua. David. Jeremiah. Daniel. Peter. Paul. To say, however, that these individuals are the sole pivots on which Bible history turns would be a serious oversimplification. These men were giants and movers, yes. But they were not always "successful." And it was not simply the force of their personalities that explains the events in which they played a part. God prepared them for their mission, and He prepared the times in which they lived. He Himself is the pivot on which history turns; God is the prime mover.

Why, then, study the lives of such men? For several reasons. Looking into their lives reminds us that even the heroes were men like us. It was God who lifted them beyond themselves, even as He can lift us beyond ourselves. Looking into their lives, we see a reflection of truths God was revealing at that particular point in time. Somehow they sum up in themselves the needs that each fresh movement of God was intended to meet. Looking into their lives, we also see more clearly how the nature of spiritual leadership differs from the autocratic Alexanders and Napoleons and Hitlers who also led men and nations.

The apostle Paul, *the* apostle in the minds of many, was one of God's movers. He was a pivot, and is so recognized in both secular and church history. He was a man in whom the issues of his time were summed up, and who in resolving them stamped his solutions on the future. But most importantly, Paul was a human being like us. In his character and personality we find a compelling portrait of the kind of person that God in Christ is inviting you and me to become.

YOUNG SAUL*

"It's a boy!"

That announcement was always welcome in a Jewish home. Saul was born in the port city of Tar-

* There have been many studies, books, and articles written about Saul. Historical details are drawn from both the Bible and other sources which tell of life in the first century A.D. Not everyone will agree with all the points presented here. Where there are differences of opinion, I have chosen to report what seems to me the most likely option rather than get bogged down in explanation and argument. Other opinions may be explored in a reference work such as the *Zondervan Pictorial Encyclopedia of the Bible.*

sus in Cilicia. It was a cosmopolitan town and an important center, a strange home for pious Jews. Saul's family may have fled there during the terrible years when the Roman armies had devastated Palestine. Financially successful, the family had won Roman citizenship. So Saul was born not only a Jew but a Roman, something in which he later took pride and which was important for his mission (Acts 22:25-29).

Saul was a product of two worlds. Committed to his Jewishness, he was still at home in the Gentile city. Throughout his life Saul would seek out the cities, those centers of communication and culture, in his driving desire to communicate the Gospel.

Saul's life, however, centered in the history of his people and his God. As was the custom, by age five Saul was learning to read and write and study the Scriptures. By ten he was taught the traditions which had grown out of generations of interpreting the Law. At thirteen he entered the community of Israel as a responsible adult, becoming a "son of the Law" (*bar mitzvah*). At that age some boys went on to deeper studies in Judaism under well-known teachers. It is a testimony both to Saul's promise and to the family wealth that he traveled to Jerusalem to study under the most famous of first-century rabbis, Gamaliel I. Already Saul had been trained both in the Scriptures and in the trade of tentmaking (for the Jews believed firmly that a scholar should labor and that a laborer should be a scholar).

Saul talked about those days in the Book of Galatians, where he shares the deep commitment that infused his passionate young heart to the strictest interpretation of Judaistic faith and life, that of the Pharisee. This very passion for God became the motive that drove him to try at first to stamp out the hated heresy of "the Way."

> For you have heard of my previous way of life in Judaism, how I violently persecuted the church of God and tried to destroy it. I was advancing in Judaism beyond many Jews of my own age and was extremely zealous for the traditions of my ancestors (Gal. 1:13, 14).

Young Saul is not a terribly attractive figure. Burning with passion, yet cold and untouched by people, this youth who had dedicated himself to the Law of Israel's God would one day, just outside Jerusalem, feel nothing but approval as waves of hatred from a maddened crowd accompanied each stone that pounded the life from the Church's first martyr, Stephen.

Saul's commitment was complete.

CONVERSION

And then came that day on the road to Damascus when Saul's whole world was jolted. The same Jesus whose followers he was planning to imprison confronted him in person! Stunned by the voice and blinded by the light that flashed around him, Saul crumpled to the ground.

At that moment, his world crumpled too. Everything that Saul had believed and the strict way of life to which he had given his passionate allegiance were suddenly revealed to be out of focus and off center. Rather than leading him to Jesus, his training and his understanding of the Old Testament had led him to reject the Lord!

It would be a decade before Saul would have all the pieces together again, but the next phase of his life would be committed completely to the one solid reality in which he could now believe. Jesus, whom Saul persecuted, was both the Lord and God's promised Christ, the Messiah. All the energies of Saul's passionate nature were focused on serving Him.

The twelve years following Saul's experience on the Damascus road are hazy. He was probably converted in A.D. 34 when he was about 34 years old. We know that he immediately began to preach Jesus as the Son of God in Damascus (Acts 9: 20). We know that within a few months he escaped a Jewish plot to murder him, and returned to Jerusalem. We know that there Barnabas brought him to the apostles, where he shared his testimony and where the reality of his conversion was recognized (Acts 9: 27). But his story was hardly more dramatic than that of many others in those days. Saul was not invited to share the leadership of the Jerusalem church.

In Jerusalem Saul's zeal in proclaiming Christ aroused anger again. It is entirely possible that the old, driving, insensitive character of the Pharisee he had been was partly responsible for this reaction, even though the attitude of the Jewish community to Christians had long since hardened. Again Saul was forced to flee for his life, and the brothers took him (perhaps protesting!) to the port city of Caesarea and "sent him off to Tarsus" (9:30).

The next ten years are obscure. In isolation the man who was God's choice to bridge two worlds, and through whom a clear formulation of the meaning of the Christian faith would be revealed, struggled to reconstruct his own picture of God and his understanding of God's ways. We can imagine him poring over the Old Testament documents, seeking illumination. We can picture him fasting and praying in the deserts of Arabia, where his final grasp of the Gospel was given to him "through a revelation of Jesus Christ" (Gal. 1:12). We can see him slipping again into Judea, not this time as the flaming evangelist of his youth, but silently seeking out the apostles to discuss with them his vision of the Gospel. After some 15 days with Peter, and a brief meeting with James, the Lord's brother, Saul went on, visiting many churches incognito as he journeyed toward home. And we can picture Saul at home again in Tarsus—waiting.

How long did he wait? How long did he walk the streets of that great trade city, watching the ships of the Mediterranean world enter the port and slip away again? How long did he sit, working thoughtfully at his trade of tentmaking?

Why didn't Saul marry during these years of waiting? He must have had opportunity. But Ananias, the man sent by God to restore the sight he lost on the road to Damascus, had shared with the new convert the Lord's announcement of his destiny: "This man is my chosen instrument to carry my name before the Gentiles and their kings and before the people of Israel" (Acts 9:15). How deeply the sight of the crowded city streets, the swirling groups of men from different lands and backgrounds, must have moved him. As a Pharisee he had formerly viewed them as dogs, deserving only contempt and hatred. Now, as a Christian, the same man was beginning to see them in a new way—as individuals with worth and value, people whom God loved.

And so Saul waited.

And then it was time for God's call.

ON MISSION

For most of the years of Saul's preparation the Church continued to be a movement within Judaism. And then at Antioch came that mass conversion of Gentiles that led to Barnabas's dispatch by the apostles to investigate. It was clear to Barnabas that the spiritual response of the Gentiles was undoubtedly a work of God. He stayed with the new believers for a time, but soon he recognized the need for help as more and more people were added to the church. Acts 11:25 tells us, "Then Barnabas went to Tarsus to look for Saul."

God had begun that work among the Gentiles for which He had been preparing the apostle.

After a happy year during which Saul shared with Barnabas and others the leadership of the church in Antioch, the two were set aside by God for the first mission to the Gentiles. We sketched that journey in our last study. By the end of that two-year trip, Saul has clearly emerged as the leader and taken a new name appropriate to his Gentile mission ("Paul," a Roman rather than a Hebrew name, means "little"). The date is early in A.D. 48.

On the missionary journey, all of Paul's studies plus the truths which he had received by direct revelation seemed to come together with exciting clarity. In the crucible of his mission, in the conflict with the Jews who followed his team and argued against him, in the questions raised by the converts, all that Paul had earlier worked out for his own peace and understanding was now applied to the Church as a whole. The old revelation and the new were not only recognized to be a unified and consistent whole, but the relationship between seemingly conflicting elements was understood. The "Gospel to the Gentiles" and the very nature of the New Testament faith and life had been worked through by this man, the Church's greatest theologian and the first apostle to the world.

Again Paul returned to Jerusalem, this time by the Holy Spirit's clear direction, to share privately with the leaders of the Jerusalem church the Gospel which he had been preaching among the Gentiles. It was just fourteen years after his conversion.

Paul discovered that the leaders there had nothing to add to his understanding. In fact, they affirmed him by recognizing his call as the apostle to the Gentiles, even as Peter was recognized as the apostle to the Jews (Gal. 2:1-10). Paul then returned to Antioch and, assured of the understanding and agreement of the other apostles and leaders in Jerusalem, began to consider the writing of a letter to the Galatians (the churches in that area which included the cities visited on the first missionary journey). The urgency of this work was highlighted by a striking incident. Peter came to visit Antioch, freely joining in fellowship with the Gentile converts. Then a party of "Judaizers" arrived. These men were believers, but believers who insisted that all Christians must adopt the Law and the Jewish life-style. When these men came, Peter refused to eat with the Gentile believers any longer!

Penetrating immediately to the tremendous significance of this issue of the Christians' relationship to the Law, Paul "opposed . . . [Peter] to his face" (Gal. 2:11). It is likely that this confrontation and the disturbing teaching of the Pharisee-Christian party led to the Jerusalem council of A.D. 49 which is recorded in Acts 15. Throughout the rest of his life Paul would accept the burden of contending for the "pure" Gospel. Through his letters you and I, too, can come to understand the uniqueness and joy of our own privilege of being a part of Christ's Church and of joining with our brothers and sisters in a full experience of the Christian life's great adventure.

PAUL, THE MAN

Eusebius records an interesting second-century description of Paul, perhaps passed on by a grandfather who had known the apostle. He was "a man small of stature, with a bald head and crooked legs, in a good state of body, with eyebrows meeting and nose somewhat hooked, full of friendliness."

91

Today it's become popular to think of Paul as a bitter and joyless man, a distant intellectual, a distorter of what Jesus taught, and a hater of women! How far from the picture the early church drew, and how far from the picture we have in Scripture. The austere Pharisee had undergone a complete transformation. The man who had cared for God in the abstract now cared for God in a deeply intimate way, and he loved people. We can't help but realize the depth of the transformation as we look at Paul's words written to the Christians in Thessalonica, recalling his time with them. His remembrance of love and intimate friendships was not written *about* a relationship, but *to* the very people who had experienced that relationship. What he writes here must be a true portrait; the Thessalonians would have immediately perceived any deceit.

We were gentle among you, like a mother caring for her little children. We loved you so much that we were delighted to share with you not only the gospel of God but our lives as well, because you had become so dear to us.

Surely you remember, brothers, our toil and hardship; we worked night and day in order not to be a burden to anyone while we preached the gospel of God to you.

You are witnesses, and so is God, of how holy, righteous and blameless we were among you who believed. For you know that we dealt with each of you as a father deals with his own children, encouraging, comforting and urging you to live lives worthy of God, who calls you into his kingdom and glory.

I Thessalonians 2:7-12

The zealot had learned to love. The Pharisee had become gentle. The man whose vision was the entire world found time for "each of you."

There are many such cameo portraits of the apostle in the New Testament. And, because in our adventure we are going to keep close company with this man and live in his letters, we need to turn to them in order to meet him as a man and to come to see him as he was. Seeing him in the intimacy of his sharing of himself, we'll also see the kind of man God can use as a spiritual leader—the kind of person that knowing Jesus frees you and me to become.

GOING DEEPER
to personalize

Examine the following passages, which give insight into Paul as a person. Then, working from the material in each, write out your answers to at least three items under 1 and 2 below. The passages are: Galatians 1, 2; Acts 9; Philippians 3; II Corinthians 1; I Thessalonians 2.

1. Impressions of Paul as a person.
    a). How did Paul relate to other people?
    b). What kind of an attitude did Paul have toward life?
    c). What were Paul's values? (What was important to him?)
    d). What were some of Paul's faults?
    e). In what ways was the older Paul unlike the younger 34-year-old?
    f). What was Paul's attitude toward himself?

g). How did Paul view his relationship with God?

2. Reactions to Paul.

    a). What is the most attractive thing to you about Paul?

    b). What do you think the people to whom he ministered thought of him?

    c). What characteristics of Paul do you think are important for spiritual leaders today? What additional qualities do you think are important?

    d). Paul wrote several times to his converts, "Imitate me, as I imitate Christ." What things about Paul do you want to imitate?

    e). How do you think Paul's enemies felt about him? Why?

to probe

1. Paul's most personal and revealing letter is the second letter to the Corinthians. Read it all, and from what you find there write a three-to-five-page paper on "Paul's way of influencing believers to respond to God."

2. Sometimes Paul is portrayed as bitterly anti-female, seeing women as "second-class citizens." In a concordance, find his every mention of *woman* and *female,* and also each place in which he refers to a woman by name. Look at *each* of these references, and write briefly how Paul viewed women both as persons and as Christians.

ANOTHER GOSPEL?

IT WAS LATE when the apostle rolled over on his pallet and saw the shafts of morning sunlight sifting through the shutters.

The confrontation over Peter's sudden unwillingness to eat with Gentile converts (Gal. 2:12) heightened Paul's awareness of the dangers facing the young Church. Then messengers had come, reporting that delegations of Christian Pharisees had visited the cities where churches had been planted. They had taught that the Gentile Christians must place themselves under the Law of Israel, and many were obeying them.

Deeply burdened, Paul had called a number of the brothers together and prayed with them through most of the night.

Now, fully awake, Paul decided to act. Filled with a deep sense of urgency, he found a pen and papyrus sheets and attacked the task he had set himself. His pen raced; passionate phrases appeared. All the churches in southern Galatia must receive a copy of this, his first letter of instruction and his first attempt to set down a theology for the new Christian movement.

"Paul an apostle–sent not from men nor by man, but by Jesus Christ" (Gal. 1:1).

These Judaizers claimed to be authorized by the Jerusalem church. As if man's authorization counted!

"I am astonished that you are so quickly deserting the one who called you by the grace of Christ and are turning to a different gospel" (1:6). Yes, God knows it *is* a different gospel! The Gospel rests solely on the grace of God. These Judaizers would make it a gospel of works-plus-faith. But works-plus-faith is not the Gospel; it is a distortion that robs the Good News of grace. It is a different, a perverted gospel!

"Am I now trying to win the approval of men, or of God? Or am I trying to please men?" (vs. 10). The gall of those Judaizers! "Paul just tried to make it easy for you," they had suggested. "He was trying to please you, afraid of your response if he didn't make the Gospel easy. But," they had continued, "there's no such thing as 'easy believism' to the Gospel. God insists that your faith cost you something!"

Paul's pen raced on. *"The gospel I preached is not something that man made up. . . . I received it by revelation from Jesus Christ"* (vss. 11,12). On and on, the words filled sheet after sheet. How exciting now to put down on paper all the deep understanding and struggles that the one-time Pharisee had spent years working through in his own life. How exciting to share with the brothers—the little children he himself had midwifed into God's Kingdom—the full

glory of what the Gospel is, and the glorious fulfillment that is offered to all who believe in Christ!

The scene just sketched is imaginary. But it must
have been much like this. It's easy to visualize Paul
pouring out his love and concern in those passionate
words to the Galatians which we read in our New
Testament.

And even today his words are so needed. Today,
too, questions arise and Christians feel concern
about the true nature of the Christian Gospel. Isn't it
a little too easy to just "accept Christ"? Can we really
say that salvation is through faith and by grace, plus
nothing? Shouldn't a Christian at least be expected to
live a certain holy life after he's come to know
Christ? Shouldn't God have a right to reject a person
who believes in Jesus but shows no respect for God
by continuing in sin?

In a later letter to the Romans (which we'll study
with the last chapters of this book) Paul goes on to
define the relationship of the Gospel to righteousness. He shows just how the Gospel produces a holy
life. But in Galatians the focal point of Paul's instruction is different. The relationship between Law and
God's grace is at issue. The question is, What lies at
the heart of the pure Gospel?

INVITATION TO *LIFE!*
Galatians 2:11-21

It's clear from both Galatians and Acts that the
confrontation between Peter and Paul in Antioch

focused on a basic issue. At that point only Paul clearly saw what that issue was.

Peter's withdrawal from Gentile believers in Antioch was hardly admirable on any basis. He once had been willing to eat and have fellowship with them. When others arrived from the Jerusalem church, Peter turned away. How deeply that must have hurt the Antioch believers! How clear an indication that they were looked on as second-class citizens of the Kingdom.

But Paul saw more than the momentary hurt. More than the hypocrisy. Paul saw the deadly intrusion of the Law into the Gospel message. Paul responded immediately, in a direct confrontation: "A man is not justified by observing the law, but by faith in Jesus Christ . . . because by observing the law no one will be justified" (vs. 16). God's verdict, declaring a person forgiven and free from the guilt and penalty of his sins, and God's power, breaking the bondage of sin to free an individual to become truly good, have nothing to do with the Law. Justification is a gift of grace, freely extended to all who put their faith in Jesus Christ.

"I do not set aside the grace of God," Paul insists, "for if righteousness could be gained through the law, Christ died for nothing!" (vs. 21).

Life. It is still a little difficult to grasp what Paul is saying. That is, until we see the key place of Galatians 2:20:

I have been crucified with Christ and I no longer live, but Christ lives in me. The life I live in the body, I live by faith in the Son of God, who loved me and gave himself for me.

Jesus' mission on earth was not to utter some new call for redoubled effort to keep the Law. Jesus' mission—and the heart of the Gospel—was to issue an invitation to life! It is tremendously dangerous to let our own focus shift from *life* to the *Law*.

Righteousness can never come through the Law. Only new life can bring us that justification from God which means both (1) entrance into a new relationship with Him and (2) the dynamic of God's power within to make possible the love, goodness, and holiness which all religions hold out as an ideal but only the Christian faith is able to provide.

With the issue clarified in his climactic statement to Peter, Paul in Galatians now launches an explosive statement contrasting the two approaches. Is the believer to work out his relationship with God through the Law or by recognizing the nature and dynamic of life? Following the argument of this letter, we discover just why the legalistic approach to the Christian life-style is doomed to failure. And we get our first glimpse of the meaning of the life principle which brings us freedom.

If you have ever felt burdened by your own Christian life or weighed down by "oughts" and "shoulds," those heavy requirements for spiritual success, then these chapters of Galatians are for you. They are the charter deed to *your* freedom and joy.

Outline. Often it helps us gain an overview of a book of the Scripture by outlining it. In outlining, we try to sum up the main point made by a writer in a paragraph or larger section of the Scripture and then show its relationship to what went before and what comes after. An outline is a tool to help us trace the writer's argument or pattern of thought.

We've seen a word outline in James. For Galatians let's look at a thought-outline, an outline that uses phrases which contain the gist of what each section teaches. Look through this outline, which covers that section of Galatians in which Paul exposes the futility of a Law approach to life. Become familiar with it, and use it when reading through the Bible text.

NOT LAW

The major portion of Galatians (outlined above) is a devastating critique of looking to the Law for help in living the Christian life.

Rather than trace through each section in detail (something you'll want to do yourself, as suggested in the GOING DEEPER study guide at the end of the chapter), let's take a look at some of the particularly significant points Paul makes:

Galatians 3:10. Paul is speaking here to "all who *rely* on observing the law" (vs. 10). He is not suggesting that the Law itself is somehow bad or wrong. But he does insist that the Law has never had anything to do with faith, and therefore reliance on the Law, either as a way of salvation or as a way to work out one's salvation, is totally inappropriate.

Paul makes an interesting point in 3:15-18. If the

100

GALATIANS 3—5
LIFE Versus LAW

Why isn't the Law for us now?

I. The Law is opposed to life (3:1-18). This is demonstrated by:
  A. Experience: How did you first receive and live your spiritual life? (3:1-5).
  B. Example: How did Old Testament saints receive spiritual life? (3:6-9).
  C. Exposition: What does the Scripture teach about how life is to be received? (3:10-18).
II. The Law's role (3:19—4:7) is shown in Scripture to be severely limited:
  A. In extent: It is temporary (3:19, 20).
  B. In ability: It cannot make alive (3:21, 22).
  C. In function: It was a custodian (3:23, 24).
  D. In force: It is nullified today (3:25—4:8).
    1. because we are "in Christ"
    2. because we are now sons
III. The Law is an inferior way that now leads to tragic results for the believer (4:8—5:12). Law leads to:
  A. Dissatisfaction: It robs us of joy (4:8-19).
  B. Bondage: It robs us of freedom (4:20—5:1).
  C. Powerlessness: It turns us from expectant faith to hopeless effort (5:2-12).

Law is so important, how did people ever get along without it? The Law wasn't even introduced until some 430 years after Abraham's day. Certainly Abraham and the other patriarchs had meaningful relationship with God!

Most important, the principle of faith in God's promise (vs. 16) was never set aside by the later introduction of the Law. Faith has always been the way to God; God's promise has never depended on the keeping of that latecomer, the Law.

101

Galatians 3:19-29 incorporates many fascinating concepts. The Law was introduced because of sin, and thus it relates to sin, not holiness. The Law was to be a *temporary* expedient, to function only until Christ came.

Picture, if you will, a raging tiger trapped behind bars. The bars were introduced because the tiger's wild impulses make him dangerous to all. Would anyone expect the *bars* to tame the tiger? Of course not! That's not the purpose of bars; they are to *restrain*. What happens then if someone does succeed in taming the tiger, using a different principle than putting him into a cage? The bars can be removed. There is no longer any use for them.

This is Paul's argument. Now that faith has come and believers have been "clothed with Christ" (vs. 27), we have been really tamed! How foolish, then, to insist that the tamed beast continue to live behind bars! Especially when all along God has affirmed His intention of removing the bars as soon as the new and living way could come (see Jer. 31:31-34).

Galatians 4:1-7. Paul uses another illustration to make this same point. It was common in the Greek culture of his day to place a young child under the supervision of a family slave, called a pedagogue (sometimes translated in vs. 2 as "guardian," "trustee," "manager," etc.). The pedagogue made sure that the child obeyed the parent, whether the child wanted to obey or not. Until the children would "receive the full rights of sons" (vs. 6) they were, in fact, no more than the slaves of a slave! They had to obey a slave who obeyed their father.

102

But then the great day came when each child was accepted as an adult. Now the father spoke directly to him. Now the son responded directly to his father. The pedagogue had no more place in their relationship.

The Law, says Paul, was a pedagogue. Jesus' redemptive act is that great event in history marking the transition from childhood to sonship. The Law, which up until Jesus had a pedagogue's purpose, now had nothing to do with our relationship with

LAW, THE PEDAGOGUE—*UNTIL* CHRIST

"No longer a slave, but a son" (Gal. 4:7)

God. "So you are no longer a slave, but a son; and since you are a son, God has made you also an heir" (vs. 7).

It is striking to see what happens when people, still fearing the tiger in them and unable to grasp the fact that Christ truly tames, seek to hide behind the bars of legalism. Such a legalism seems at first to promise a certain kind of security. The bars not only keep us in; they also keep others out.

But Christ's people are not made to cower in barred caves and cages! We have been shaped by God to live on the plains and mountains and, yes, in the jungles of the whole wide world. Jesus Himself set us the example. He stepped boldly from the security of Heaven and was caught up in the rush and swirl, the joys and agonies, of human experience. He entered the homes of publicans and sinners, enjoyed the wedding parties, reached out to touch and heal the hurting, and confronted the hardened Pharisees. Jesus was totally involved—yet uncontaminated. He rubbed shoulders with sinners—and remained pure. He lived with and like other men—and revealed God. His whole life was an adventure.

It is to just this kind of adventure that you and I are called today. Jesus did **not** come to bring a new set of bars for our cage. He came to tame our tigers and to release us to live as He Himself lived in the world of men. The meaning of our life, the adventure of it, isn't to be found in the cages Christians make for themselves and decorate so attractively. No, meaning and joy for us are to be found in stepping outside the old cages, dismissing the no-longer-needed pedagogues, and setting out into the future to live as *sons*.

All too often, though, we draw back.

We fear.

We don't realize that as God's sons we now have His life. Like the Judaizers of Paul's day, we hurriedly try to shape new bars as fast as God tears them down. In deepest agony Paul cried out to the cage-builders of his day, "How is it that you are turning back to those weak and miserable principles? Do you wish to be enslaved by them all over again?" (4: 9).

You will lose your joy! (4: 15).

You will lose your freedom! (5: 1).

You will lose your power (5: 4). You will lose all that Jesus died to make available for you as you live your new life now.

Galatians 5: 4. It is important to realize that here Paul is focusing on present-tense salvation, not on past-tense (see pp. 42-44). What Paul means when he says that those who "are trying to be justified by law have been alienated from Christ; you have fallen away from grace" (vs. 4) must be seen in the context of the passage.

Paul has shown that the Law was a pedagogue. Once the Law was the avenue through which a believer experienced his relationship with God. But now the relationship is direct and personal, as with a child who at last did "receive the full rights of sons" (4: 5). What, then, if a son keeps going back to his old pedagogue for directions? Clearly he has alienated himself from the personal relationship. Such a fall

105

from grace back into old practices and ways and attitudes means that the individual is no better off than he was before! All the freedom, all the joy, and all the adventure of a life lived as a child of God have been lost—traded away for worse than nothing. Of course, "Christ will be of no value to you at all" (vs. 2). What *difference* will being a Christian make? None. You will be no better off now than before.

NO BETTER OFF

This seems like a hard thing to say. No better off? Why, Heaven has been won, at least! Yes, but the Christian faith is not something solely concerned with eternity. The Christian faith includes God's affirmation that your life *now* is important as well— important to God, important to others, and important to you.

The great adventure that God offers you and me in Christ provides solid hope and the expectation of meaning and joy and fulfillment today. Have you been missing it? Have you believed "for Heaven" and failed to realize that God wants to give you the joy of it each day? If you have missed the joy of your salvation, it may be because, as is true with so many others, you've continued to sit behind the bars of cages God long ago unlocked, behind doors He long ago flung open wide.

Rethink your life.

Explore with Paul the emptiness of the Law.

And step outside where the horizons stretch beyond the gaze of even the most piercing eye.

GOING DEEPER

We've just begun our exploration of the relationship between the believer and the Law. This study will take us to the end of this book as we trace the Bible's teaching in both Galatians and Romans. So don't expect everything to become clear this first week. Instead, concentrate on what this section of the Scripture teaches, and master it. Soon all will come together in a harmonious whole.

to personalize

1. What are some "laws" (customs, rules, etc.) you have relied on to help you be a better Christian? Have they helped you? How? Have they harmed? How?

2. Which of the following do you think Paul would see as legalistic? Have reasons for your choices.
   a) A Christian ought to be in church twice on Sunday.
   b) A Christian should witness to everyone he meets.
   c) A Christian should not associate with people who curse and swear.
   d) A Christian should read the Bible and pray daily.

3. Read Galatians 3:1—5:12 carefully, guided by the outline on page 101. When you have finished, try to say in a single paragraph what Paul is presenting.

4. On the following continuum lines, put a check

107

mark at the place which best indicates where you are now:

    a) Compared to last year, I now feel more free.
    True _____False
    b) Compared to last year, I now feel more fulfilled.
    True _____False
    c) Compared to last year, I now have more joy.
    True _____False
    d) I consider myself to be a legalistic person.
    True _____False
    e) Compared to last year, Jesus is far more real to me.
    True _____False

5. Now redo the same five continuum questions two times on a separate sheet of paper. *First,* fill them in as you think the apostle Paul would have when he wrote Galatians. *Second,* fill them in as you think the Galatian people would have.

6. Compare the three patterns (yours, Paul's, the Galatians'). What observations do you make? What conclusions do they seem to suggest?

UNCAGED

FOR THE FIRST TIME in his life, Jim found himself wildly cursing. The vicious words poured out, fed by a rage that both frightened and exhilarated him. His face twisted with anger, Jim shouted out words that he had always been ashamed even to think.

"Good! Good!" encouraged the young professor when Jim's rage finally collapsed in sudden exhaustion. "Jim, you're really learning to express your feelings. The real you is finally surfacing!"

This scene is imaginary, but it has been repeated many times. The young professor represents one particular school of psychological therapy group training. "We're only allowed to talk about the here and now. And we're going to learn to express what we really feel. So whatever you feel—about yourself, about anyone else here—I want you to express it openly and honestly."

Such instructions are designed to break through the barriers of convention that cause people to repress their feelings and to help them find a kind of release. The notion seems to be that by bringing negative feelings out into the open, the person will rid himself of them. Or at least he will learn to accept and to handle them. Somehow this process is supposed to give a new freedom to individuals to find themselves and to grow.

This is *not* a picture of Christian freedom. Such excesses can turn us away from the whole idea of freedom. Some of us are frightened to discover that God has now taken away the bars of the Law and has left us uncaged. No wonder we, like the Galatians, rush to build new cages! We not only seek safety from a hostile world, but we just as desperately try to place restraints on our hostile selves. We know only too well the hidden thoughts and motives, the secret desires, that we struggle to keep buried. And so we're afraid. If the bars of the Law are taken away, won't something terrible in us be released?

FREEDOM

The Bible insists, "It is for freedom that Christ has set us free" (5:1). Scripture is not speaking of the kind of freedom the young professor was encouraging. "Do not use your freedom to indulge your sinful nature," Paul explains. "Rather, serve one another in love" (Gal. 5:13). Christian freedom is designed to help us grow in goodness.

Let's be sure of one thing. In affirming freedom, the Christian is not expressing a desire to release sinful passions. In affirming freedom, the Christian

110

responds to God's own call to shake off old bonds and to find His new pathway to goodness. The Law throughout its history never succeeded in producing righteousness. We are to look beyond the Law now—to a better way.

The group therapy offered Jim a counterfeit freedom. Encouragement to express anger and other negative feelings (in order to "get rid of" them) has been shown to produce just the opposite of the desired effect. The more a person expresses hostility. the more deeply he seems to feel it. And the more quickly he interprets others' actions as a cause for anger. For a person without Christ in a society of people who do not respond to God, the Law's restraints are both wise and necessary. Unchecked, the tiger within man does quickly take control.

But there is a basic difference between the believer who has established a personal relationship with God through faith and the unbeliever who has not. The Christian is no longer under the Law because, unlike other men, he can now "live by the Spirit" (5:16). An entirely new principle of life governs and guides the believer and provides a basis for his freedom.

Made alive. One of the most exciting themes in Scripture is that of life. In Genesis we see God giving life to all His creation. We see Him breathing a special life into Adam and Eve: physical life, and more! They were spiritually alive, aware of God, capable of fellowship with Him.

When Adam and Eve chose sin, they died spiritu-

111

ally (Gen. 2:17). This spiritual death was passed on to their children and became the one great devastating flaw in mankind. Dimly aware of God and goodness, man's spiritual deadness leads him to respond to the self-centered drives of his sin-warped nature rather than to God. "As for you, you were dead in your transgressions and sins," Paul wrote later in Ephesians (2:1). "All of us lived among them at one time, gratifying the cravings of our sinful nature and following its desires and thoughts. Like the rest, we were by nature objects of wrath" (2:3).

Man the sinner needs both human law and divine Law. Without restraint, with each individual given license to express his cravings, society would fall and individuals would prey on those weaker than they and, in turn, be a prey to the stronger.

If we think this picture is exaggerated, we are ignorant of history. The wars, the rapes, the murders, the systematic crimes of economic oppression, the private brutalities—all fill in the details of man's Fall. The very fear which so many feel when one speaks of freedom from the Law's restraint is adequate testimony that, deep down, each of us is already aware of man's depravity—by being aware of our own.

But the Bible story does not stop at death. The Bible goes on to share the Good News of *life!* God "made us alive with Christ even when we were dead in transgressions" (Eph. 2:5). When we come by faith into a relationship with Jesus Christ, God plants His own new life in our personality. All the New Testament writers speak of it. Peter, the other

112

apostle on whom the Book of Acts focuses, puts it this way, "For you are not just mortals now but sons of God: the live, permanent Word of the living God has given you his own indestructible heredity" (I Pet. 1:23, Phillips). There is a new kind of life swelling up within the Christian. It is God's kind of life, and our possession of God's life changes everything.

We wisely are afraid to remove the restraints from our old selves.

But who feels a need to restrain God?

The Spirit. Now we will begin to penetrate to the root of the great adventure.

Six times in these next few verses of Galatians (5:16-25) Paul speaks of the Holy Spirit:

"Live by the Spirit" (vs. 16).

"The Spirit . . . is contrary to the sinful nature" (vs. 17).

"Led by the Spirit, . . . not under law" (vs. 18).

"The fruit of the Spirit is . . . " (vs. 22).

"We live by the Spirit . . . " (vs. 25a).

"Keep in step with the Spirit" (vs. 25b).

The dynamic of Christian freedom is found not only in the possession of new life but also in the person of the Holy Spirit. God Himself has entered us with His gift of power.

In affirming freedom, Paul is not telling us to let the old nature go in an orgy of selfish self-expression. Instead Paul is asking us to trust ourselves to God the Holy Spirit and to look to Him alone to express through us that quality of life that is both new and His own.

Only if the tiger in me is truly tamed do I dare take the bars away. With new life and through the Holy Spirit's power I can at last find the courage to be free.

GALATIANS 5:13-22

This vital and exciting passage contains Paul's explanation of what he meant when he wrote in Galatians 2:20, "I no longer live, but Christ lives in me. The life I live in the body, I live by faith in the Son of God, who loved me and gave himself for me." Paul found freedom not to be "himself" but to be his *new* self. And Paul recognized that new life as God's own.

Galatians 5:13-15. We are never to mistake Christian freedom for the kind of liberty the therapy group tried to give Jim. Christian freedom is always in harmony with the Law, although it does not rely on the Law. The Law does show us one aspect of the way of love.

The problem with the Law is that it cannot *produce* love. But the Law can still warn us if we misuse our freedom to "bite and devour" (v. 15) one another.

Galatians 5:16-18. The Holy Spirit is not motivated by the cravings of a sin nature. So the issue facing us now is simply this: Will we surrender ourselves to Him? If we do let the Spirit guide and control us, then He will see to it that we do not "gratify the desires of [our] sinful nature" (vs. 16).

The issue, Paul is saying again, *has nothing to do* with the Law.

Galatians 5:19-21. All those things which the Law

GALATIANS 5
FREEDOM TO LIVE

"sinful nature" (death)   **"Spirit" (new life)**

Characteristics

"sinful nature" (death)	"Spirit" (new life)
* not responsive to God	* responsive to God
* in conflict with the Spirit	* in conflict with the sinful nature
* ruled by its cravings	* ruled by God

Products

immorality	love
impurity	joy
debauchery	peace
idolatry and witchcraft	patience
hatred	kindness
discord	goodness
jealousy	faithfulness
fits of rage	gentleness
selfish ambition	self-control
dissensions	
factions	
envy	
drunkenness	
orgies	

Relationship to the Law

The Law is "against such things" (5:23) and was added "because of transgressions" (3:19).	NONE. "Against such there is no law" (5:22).

---

speaks out against and is designed to protect society from are listed here. They are seen to flow from man's sinful nature. As long as the desires of our sinful nature are in control, our character and behavior will be marked by these products.

115

Galatians 5:22-26. The Holy Spirit also produces fruit in human life—fruit in stark contrast to that of the sinful nature. Love, joy, peace—all those things we yearn for—come as we keep in step with the Spirit of God. And no law was ever passed against love!

GALATIANS 6:1-18

The last chapter of this early New Testament letter contains several injunctions and personal greetings. The brothers are encouraged not to deal harshly with those who are learning to walk the new life (6:1, 2). One who falls should be restored gently. Each brother should seek to help others along the way and fulfill Christ's new commandment to love (Jn. 13:33, 34). Recognizing the divine source of the new life, each man can rejoice in his own gifts and actions without that kind of pride that comes from feeling better than someone else (Gal. 6:3-5).

In all of life's adventures, we can live in total honesty with ourselves and with God. We will never deceive ourselves into believing that Christian freedom is a license to sin (6:7-10). We can always commit ourselves to doing good, sure that "at the proper time we will reap a harvest" (vs. 9) in joy.

Summing up (6:12-18), Paul again points us to the cross of Jesus Christ, where He (and each believer, too!) was crucified. Jesus died—but He rose again. In Him, you and I have risen as well to a new life in a new world. It is a world not ruled by the old Law but one filled with the vital presence of God Himself. In this new world "neither circumcision nor uncircumcision means anything" (6:15). Jew and Gentile meet at the cross, and at the cross each abandons his old life-style and culture to find in Christ's new creation a new and living way.

GOING DEEPER
to personalize

1. This short but significant section of Scripture introduces a theme developed at length in Romans. There are several key words and concepts to master. Look over Galatians 5, and jot down a single sentence which expresses your own understanding at this time of how each of these terms relates to this theme:

- freedom
- the Spirit
- new creation
- sinful nature
- fruit

2. In Galatians 5:16-25 there are several statements of how believers are to relate to the Holy Spirit. (Again, our study of Romans will make many of these ideas much more clear.) For now, jot down what you understand each to indicate or mean.
- Live by the Spirit (v. 16).
- Led by the Spirit (v. 18).
- Keep in step with the Spirit (v. 25).

3. In Galatians 5:22, 23, Paul says of the qualities produced by the Holy Spirit, "Against such there is no law."
  a) Why do you think this phrase is added here?
  b) Most of the Ten Commandments are

phrased "Thou shalt not." Why do you think God chose this negative phrasing rather than the more positive "thou shalt"?

c) Think. Is the Law always negative?

4. See how well you grasp the three different approaches to life represented by Paul in Galatians. Do this by writing three first-person accounts. Each account should express how the supposed writer acts and feels and behaves, showing what his or her approach to life implies. The three people whose accounts you will write are:

Jack. Jack is a libertarian. To Jack, freedom means "I do what I want when I want."

Jenny. Jenny is a legalist. To Jenny, thoughts of freedom are frightening. She looks to a long list of thou-shalt-not's to protect her from herself and others.

Jan. Jan is a Christian who has grasped the new-creation dimension of life in Christ and is growing in His kind of freedom.

Be ready to read one or more of these accounts to your class or home-study group.

RIGHTEOUSNESS NOW?

"BUT THAT MEANS YOU CAN DO ANYTHING you want to and still go to Heaven!"

I heard that objection often from my navy buddies. Faith alone the way to salvation? No careful keeping of the divine Law as an additional requirement? Then, what is to keep a person from going out and sinning as much as he pleases? It all sounded so ridiculous to them. Didn't God care about righteousness anymore?

This is how Paul's teaching in Galatians must have seemed to some who fixed only upon his argument against the Law and missed the implications of chapter 5. If God releases believers from the Law, then He must have retreated from His concern for righteousness. To most people, the Law and righteousness seem inseparably linked.

Some years after writing Galatians, the great apostle wrote another letter to another young church. This church had formed in Rome, the center of the empire itself. In his letter to the Romans, Paul answers the questioners of his day and the uncertain people of ours. His answer is a careful explanation of how the Gospel is related to righteousness—both God's righteousness and our own.

ROME

As early as the second century B.C., a Jewish colony existed in Rome. After 63 B.C., when Judea became a part of the Roman Empire, this colony grew. By 59 B.C., Cicero writes of it as powerful and influential.

At times the Jews suffered expulsion from the city, as in an A.D. 19 financial scandal. Yet, within a few years the Jews would drift back again to this center of finance, trade, and political power. In A.D. 49 Claudius expelled the Jews from Rome in an act mentioned in Acts 18:2. Strikingly, the historian Suetonius says that the cause of Claudius' action was the "constant indulgence of the Jews in riots at the instigation of one Chrestus." Apparently the message of Christ divided the Jewish community at Rome and, as it did in the cities to which Paul journeyed on his missions, provoked a bitter and violent controversy. Priscilla and Aquila, whom we meet later in this letter and who are mentioned in Acts 18, were apparently converted at this time. They were already believers when Paul met them.

Claudius' expulsion edict, like the earlier ones, had no lasting effect. A few years later the Jewish colony flourished again and, as before, included Jewish believers in Jesus. By the time Paul wrote his letter to the Romans, a large number of Gentile and Jewish Christians comprised a typical church.

Paul had longed to go to Rome, both to minister to the believers there and to be encouraged by them. But he was not able to go just then. So instead he sent a lengthy letter. In his letter we have our most careful, thorough, and detailed explanation of that Gospel which God called Paul to preach. In Galatians we catch glimpses of themes that Paul now fully develops. As we study Romans, we see that in Christ God has truly taken a new and dynamic approach to the question of righteousness. The cage of the Law was designed to restrain *unrighteousness.* The freedom of the Gospel is designed to *produce in man the righteousness of our God!* "In the gospel," Paul affirms, "a righteousness from God is revealed, a righteousness that is by faith from first to last" (1:17).

This, too, is God's gift to us.

To adventure in *righteousness.*

Not by the Law.

But by faith.

Outline. This verse (1:17) states the theme of Romans and gives us the key to outlining the book. For convenience, this outline is organized under five major headings.

ROMANS
Revealing Righteousness from God

I. Introduction (1:1-17)
   A. Salutation (1-7)
   B. Personal items (8-13)
   C. Theme (14-17)

121

II. Deliverance: Righteous standing a gift (1:18—5:21)
   A. Universal need of righteousness (1:18—3:21)
      1. Guilt of the Gentiles (1:18-32)
      2. Guilt of the Jews (2:1—3:8)
      3. Proof of universal guilt (3:9-20)
   B. Provision of Righteousness (3:21-26)
   C. Harmonization: Justification and the Law (3:27-31)
   D. Illustration: Justification in the Old Testament (4:1-25)
      1. Abraham, David, and justification (1-8)
      2. Circumcision and justification (9-12)
      3. Inheritance and justification (13-17)
      4. Faith and justification (18-25)
   E. Exaltation: The certainty of justification (5:1-11)
   F. Summation: The universality of justification (5:12-21)
III. Victory: Righteous living a possibility (6:1—8:39)
   A. The basis for victory: Union with Christ (6:1-14)
   B. The principle: Enslaved to righteousness (6:15-23)
   C. The relationship: Freed from the Law (7:1-25)
      1. Law and the believer (7:1-6)
      2. Law and sin (7:7-12)
      3. Indwelling sin and the believer (7:13-25)
   D. The Power: The Spirit within (8:1-17)
   E. The End: Glorification (8:18-39)
IV. History: Righteous dealings a certainty (9:1—11:36)
   A. Israel's present rejection is just (9:1-33)
   B. Israel's present rejection explained (10:1-21)
   C. Israel's present rejection not complete (11:1-36)
      1. It is not total (11:1-10)
      2. It is not final (11:11-36)
V. Community: A righteous reality (12-16)
   A. Christ's interpersonal impact (12, 13)
      1. In the community (12:1-21)
      2. In society (13:1-14)
   B. Christ's attitude incarnated (14:1—15:13)
      1. Uncondemning (14:1-13)
      2. Self-sacrificing (14:13—15:4)
      3. Purposive (15:5-13)
   C. Paul's farewells (15:14—16:27)

In tracing through the Book of Romans then, you and I find an exciting picture of the life to which God has called us. The Christian adventure means for us a life of:
- Deliverance
- Victory
- Community

A life lived with a complete confidence in the God who has worked through all of history to bring us, and all mankind, the rich benefits of His righteousness and love.

DELIVERANCE
Romans 1–5

As Paul penned these first chapters, one reality dominated his thought. It is a theme with which he concludes this section in chapter 5. "By the trespass of the one man [Adam], death reigned" (5:17). We must begin our understanding of salvation with the fact of man's deadness.

All too often men have begun their thinking about their relationship with God with a different assumption. To some, a man seems born with spiritual life and forfeits that life only when he personally chooses sin. Others believe that a man is born neutral. To them the issue remains in doubt until the final judgment when acts will be weighed in a set of divine balances. If, at that time, there is more good than bad, so the thinking goes, eternal life will be the reward.

Paul has no such image of man. Taking seriously

the Old Testament picture of the Fall, Paul is convinced that all human beings are born spiritually
dead and alienated from God. Both by nature and
by choice, human beings willingly choose sin, even
when they know the good. The basic question which
then must be answered is, How do we receive life?

This is a question Paul himself never asked or
even thought of in his early years. As a young
Pharisee, the 30-year-old Saul assumed that life was
his and that he could please God by a rigorous keeping of the Law. Only later, jolted by the appearance
of Jesus on the road to Damascus, did Saul go back to
probe the untested assumptions on which his whole
life had been based.

Now, writing to the Romans, Paul realizes that
there will be many others like himself who have not
traced the implications of faith in Jesus back to the
basics. So in the first three chapters particularly,
Paul seeks to demonstrate the deadness of mankind.
We do not die spiritually because of sin, Paul
teaches. Instead, our sins demonstrate our deadness. It is because we are spiritually dead and desperately in need of life that we live the warped way
we do.

Thus man's basic need is not for the Law to show
him how to live. Man's need is life itself—and life is
not communicated through the Law.

Romans 1:18-32. Paul is familiar with the sinful
life-style seen in pagan society and also in the stories
of pagan gods and goddesses. The Gentiles have not
come to this depraved state because they had no
opportunity to know God. Paul says that ever since

Creation, God's invisible qualities have "been clearly seen" (1:20). What can be known about God through nature "is plain to them" (vs. 19).

No, the fact of mankind's depravity is shown in that, confronted by God, "they neither glorified him as God nor gave thanks to him" (vs. 21). This reaction against God when contact is made by Him (like the reaction of a hand against a hot stove) is a convincing demonstration of man's spiritual condition. To contact God—the Bible's God of love and righteousness—and to be repelled! And then to choose all sorts of corruption and wickedness rather than Him! How plainly such a people must be both guilty and dead.

Romans 2:1–3:8. Now Paul suddenly turns on the Jewish reader who has been applauding his devastating critique of Gentile lostness. The Jew is proud that he knows more about God than the Gentile. He has received God's Law! But *knowing* good means nothing: It is *doing* that counts (2:7-11). In fact, the possessors of the Law "who brag about the law" have throughout history been those who "dishonor God by breaking the law" (2:23). The pagans see the hypocrisy of God's people, and "God's name is blasphemed among the Gentiles because of you" (2:24).

Romans 2:14, 15 is an interesting aside which has often been misunderstood. Paul points out that the Jews, recipients of the revealed Law, are not the only ones with moral standards. The Gentiles too have a moral nature, a conscience that leads them to set up standards of right and wrong by which to judge themselves and others. "By nature" they do what the

125

whole concept of the Law requires: measure, evaluate, and condemn or attempt to excuse. When God's judgment day comes, both Jew and Gentile will be shown to fall short of whatever standards each approves.

This is a helpful insight for those who are honestly concerned about God's "unfairness" in failing to reveal His standards of right and wrong to everybody. God will not judge pagans by Scripture's standards of right and wrong. He will judge all men by their own standards. But it will make no difference, for all will fall short.

The failure of individuals and societies to live up to the standards they themselves recognize is additional evidence that men are both lost and dead. There is no help for us in ourselves.

Romans 3:9-20. Having made the charge that Jew and Gentile alike are "all under sin," Paul now brings together a collage of Old Testament verses to provide proof. The evidence of history and personal experience is impressive. The statements of God in His Word are conclusive.

Given, then, the lost and sinful state in which men live, what can we say about the Law? Simply that the Law must be understood to have one and only one function as far as sinful man is concerned. The Law, God's statement of His righteousness in the form of standards by which men can be commanded to live, *is designed to make us "conscious of sin"* (vs. 20). No one who honestly looks at himself and his behavior in the light of God's righteous commands can be left with any illusions. "Whatever the law says, it says to those

126

who are under the law, so that every mouth may be silenced and the whole world held accountable to God. Therefore no one will be declared righteous in his sight by observing the law; rather, through the law, we become conscious of sin" (vss. 19, 20).

Romans 3:21-26. Paul now turns to the Gospel. God has made known a "righteousness from God, apart from law" (vs. 21). "This righteousness from God comes through faith in Jesus Christ to all who believe" (vs. 22) with no difference made between Gentile and Jew, for all have sinned. The basis on which righteousness is offered is the blood of Christ, poured out as a "sacrifice of atonement" (vs. 25). Salvation rests on the work of God in Christ; there is no human contribution. God's grace, His free choice to *give* what we do not have and cannot earn, is at the root of salvation. All God asks from man is faith.

Paul also notes here that the cross demonstrates not only God's grace but also His justice. In the past, too, God offered forgiveness. But how could a holy God let sin go unpunished? The cross reveals a God who does not relax His standards. The penalty which justice demands—death for the sinner—was paid by God Himself. Grace and forgiveness do not come cut-rate. The price was the blood of the Son.

Romans 3:27-31. To all who object that this robs the Law of honor, Paul responds, "Never!"

The principle of faith excludes boasting, yes. It makes salvation's offer accessible to all, yes. But it also upholds the role of the Law (the role that God gave the Law, not the role mistakenly given it by men). The Law's place is established as the revealer of man's lostness, as a compelling call to look to Christ for a righteousness which can come only as God's gift through faith.

Romans 4:1-8. The Jewish reader or the Gentile believer who has become familiar with the Old Testament will immediately ask how this "New Testament notion" of faith squares with the total revelation of God's dealings with men. Quickly Paul points out that Abraham was himself justified by faith: "Abraham believed God, and it was credited to him as righteousness" (4: 3). David, too, is among those Old Testament saints who understood that a relationship with God is a matter of faith rather than works: "Blessed is the man whose sin the Lord will never count against him" (4: 8).

These two quotes point up important features of a key theological term introduced here and in Galatians: *justification* (see p. 98).

Justification as a theological word reflects the fact that, on the basis of Christ's death, God judicially pronounces righteous the person who believes in Him. His faith, like Abraham's, is accepted in place of righteousness, and then righteousness is credited to his account. On the one hand, justification involves forgiveness of sins. On the other hand, justification involves *imputing* Christ's own righteousness to the believer. The Augsburg Confession (Art. 21) explains imputation this way: "As when my friend pays the debt for a friend, the debtor is freed by the merit of another, as though it were by his own. Thus, the merits of Christ are bestowed upon us."

This concept of *justification by faith,* Paul shows, is

not just a New Testament idea. It goes back to the spiritual experience of the very founder of the Hebrew commonwealth.

Romans 4:9-12. The promise that Abraham received by faith came *before* the sign of circumcision was introduced. The true relationship with God always rested on *faith alone.*

Romans 4:13-17. The promise was given to Abraham and his children. It must be received by us in the same way that Abraham received it: "by faith" (vs. 13). All who, like Abraham, place their trust in God, are guaranteed a place in God's family. Through faith we enter that same relationship with God into which Abraham, the forefather of all who believe, entered.

Romans 4:18-24. Abraham's faith, portrayed in the Old Testament, helps us understand the nature of faith in Christ. Abraham was given a promise which it seemed impossible for God to keep. Yet "he did not waver through unbelief" (vs. 20). Abraham was "fully persuaded that God had power to do what he had promised" (vs. 21). This unwavering confidence in God as a trustworthy Person is the saving faith which is accepted in place of the righteousness we do not possess. Righteousness is ours today, as it was Abraham's, when we place our confidence in God's Son, Jesus Christ, fully persuaded that "he was delivered over to death for our sins and was raised to life for our justification" (vs. 25).

Romans 5:1-11. Paul's reasoning has led now to an exciting climax. Justified by faith, we have peace with God. We have access. We have *hope* (which, in the Bible, is a word of certainty and expectation, not doubt!). We know that the God who was willing to die for us when we were still His enemies will certainly guarantee the ultimate deliverance of all who through faith enter into a personal relationship with Him.

Paul invites us, as believers, to realize the endless welcome we have from our Father and to "rejoice in God through our Lord Jesus Christ, through whom we have now received reconciliation" (vs. 11).

Romans 5:12-21. Now, summing up the impact of these early chapters of Romans, Paul fashions his summary around the theme of life and death. In Adam, death came to all men. Death reigned from Adam to Moses; no law was required to bring spiritual death. Death is the condition of all, a condition that the Law merely reveals.

Then came Jesus. And Jesus, the second Adam, brought to all men the gift of life. That one act of His in dying for man's sin is God's abundant provision for the lost race. Through Jesus, there is now available to all the "justification that brings life for all men" (vs. 18).

Not all men accept the gift.

But the gift is offered to all.

Life. Forgiveness. Righteousness. And for each one who goes on to live in God's grace: adventure.

GOING DEEPER
to personalize

1. Read through Romans 1—5 carefully, guided

by the outline on pages 121-122. As you read, jot down any questions you may have.

2. Go back over the chapters again, making a list of everything from which God offers deliverance. Which of these seems most important to you?

3. Look in the newspaper to find modern-day evidence that mankind is spiritually dead and in rebellion against God (see, for example, the list in Rom. 1:18-32).

4. How would you answer a person who is concerned that the lost have "no chance" because they have not heard of Jesus? (See 1:18-21; 2:12-16.)

5. In your own words, explain the "function of the Law *as far as sinful man is concerned*" (3:19, 20).

6. From Romans 4, develop a two-page description of faith. What is faith? What difference does it make? What is faith based on? What is the object of faith (e.g., the *content* which is to be believed)? What is the outcome of faith? Be as careful and thorough as you can, but study *only* Romans 4 and the Old Testament passages cited there as your sources.

7. Romans 5:1-11 speaks of the confidence that believers can have in their "by faith" relationship with God. Study the passage, and *list everything of which Paul feels sure* (and which is a cause of his rejoicing). Which of these is most important to you personally?

to probe

1. Read at least one commentary discussion of the background of the letter to the Romans.

2. If you are taking this course for credit, begin

now to *memorize* the outline of Romans. It will help you develop a mastery of this key New Testament book.

3. Select one key verse from each of the first five chapters of Romans. Choose those which seem to you to epitomize the contribution of each chapter to Paul's argument. Be prepared to defend your choices.

4. Romans 5: 12-21 is a difficult passage for theology. Read and compare at least three different commentaries on this passage. Make a list of the points on which all commentators agree. Next, make a list of issues on which they differ. Then write a three-page summary statement explaining the teaching of this section of Scripture as you understand it.

PEACE WITH GOD

I REMEMBER how guilty I felt.

A young teenager, I'd traced pictures of female underwear models from the Sears catalog and hidden the "pinups" under my mattress. When mom changed the sheets, she found them. And left them, exposed on top of my bed.

Burning with shame, I'd tried to brazen it through. With attempted enthusiasm, I hurried out to the back garden to offer my help to dad, who was trimming a peach tree.

There were other times I felt guilt, too. Like the time John Weimer and I picked the only plum on the new tree just before it ripened. Mom had been heartbroken; she'd looked forward so much to tasting that one plum. John and I hadn't even eaten it! We'd opened it and thrown the still-hard flesh of the plum on our garage floor.

Guilt. Sometimes it's because of willful choice of what is known to be wrong. Sometimes it's for unwitting failures. Either way, to feel guilty is pure agony, to recognize our own failure and inadequacy.

Feelings of guilt are common in our society. Sometimes our feelings are rooted in specific acts. A spouse is unfaithful. A mother neglects a young child who is later injured. A teenager lies to his parents about where he is going. A businessman cheats on a contract.

Sometimes feelings of guilt are rooted in the growing awareness that we are unable to cope with life. We fall short over and over again. Somehow we must be to blame. The sense of guilt grows. Plagued by the awareness of our failures and inadequacy, we may try several different approaches to freedom.

■ One approach to handling guilt is to deny it. Our feelings of guilt, we say, come from hang-ups that society imposes on us. So we insist that everyone has the right to do his own thing, that there are no absolute moral standards binding on us.

■ Another approach to handling guilt is to explain it away. We look back into our childhood and find reasons why we couldn't help ourselves from making some of the choices we did. Often criminal behavior is explained away as being due to the societal conditions rather than the individual's choice. Denying personal responsibility is a popular way to approach the problem of guilt.

■ A third approach to handling guilt is to construct a system of do's and don'ts which we *can* live up to. Then we reassure ourselves of our own goodness by meticulously keeping the laws we build. This legalistic approach, which features constant comparison of

ourselves with others to demonstrate how much better we are, is a favorite approach of the religious.
▪ Yet another approach to handling guilt is this: enjoy sin! The first pangs of conscience will recede if we throw ourselves into the pursuit of sinful pleasures. With our consciences seared, we'll not be troubled by guilt anymore.

GUILTY

There are other approaches as well. But each of them crumbles when, as in Romans 3, we hear the shouted verdict of the Law. The Law speaks so that "every mouth may be stopped and all the world may become guilty before God" (3: 19, KJV). With God's Law comes the consciousness of sin.

Guilt is such a big thing with us, felt intensely by so many, that it is hard to grasp the fact that the Bible does not speak of guilt feelings! Instead, Scripture speaks only of real guilt: responsibility incurred by sin itself. Even here, guilt is hardly a dominant Bible theme. *Young's Analytical Concordance* lists only six New Testament references to guilt or guiltiness, and of the seventeen Old Testament references, eight of them are found in Leviticus 4—6, the explanation of the sin offerings through which guilt would be covered.

God seems far more interested in speaking to us of forgiveness than of guilt!

The most frequently used Old and New Testament words that speak of forgiveness have the same root meaning: to send away. In each case what is sent away is not the feelings of guilt that flow from our acts of sin or our inadequacy, but the sin itself. It is the *sin* that is forgiven or sent away. This act of God in forgiving through Jesus is the source of a new freedom for us. The New Testament quotes an Old Testament promise: "I will forgive their wickedness, and will remember their sins no more" (Heb. 8:12). In another place this is repeated: "Their sins and lawless acts I will remember no more" (Heb. 10:17). Because of Jesus, our sins have been dealt with fully and completely. As far as God is concerned, the issue is settled. Forgiveness is so complete that sins are no longer even remembered.

Then what of guilt? *Because sins are dealt with and "sent away," we are no longer guilty!* We stand uncondemned before God! Justified by faith, we now "have peace with God through our Lord Jesus Christ" (Rom. 5:1, KJV).

Guilt feelings? Sometimes guilt feelings linger on after we have accepted forgiveness. This is one of the things we will learn to overcome as we grow in our Christian experience. A child frightened by a dog may grow up to be terrified of even the tiniest poodle. The fear remains, dominating his reactions, even after all reason for such fear is gone. Often Christians have guilt reactions long after forgiveness has removed their cause. Each new failure may frighten, and we may react in one of the old ways in a desperate attempt to handle the guilt feelings. What we need to do is to realize that *forgiveness* is God's way of dealing with our *every* sin. In Jesus we *have* forgiveness.

As forgiven men and women, we have release from guilt and are at peace with God.

And at peace with ourselves.

Peace? To many this kind of peace may seem inadequate. Why doesn't God deal with sin before we commit it rather than simply promise forgiveness after each new failure? The exciting victory message of Romans 6—8 is: *God does!* The death of Christ provides both peace and power.

To grasp what we're about to read there, we need to clarify one or two points about sin. Scripture speaks of sin both as (1) a "nature" and as (2) actions. In the first sense, *sin* speaks of man's spiritual deadness that warps the human personality, which is expressed in sinful acts. As a word describing the human condition, *sin* indicates that human beings both desire and willingly choose to do things which are evil. Not everyone will choose the gross sins, but each person will be moved by selfish passions and concerns rather than by God's kind of love for others and for goodness.

Man's sinful actions are portrayed in the Bible as the fruit or expression of his warped nature. Our sins do not make us sinful. Instead, our sins demonstrate the fact that sinfulness is already a human characteristic!

It's clear, then, that if God is to act in our lives to deal with the sin question, He must offer more than forgiveness. If Christ's death *really* dealt with sin, then redemption must affect the sin nature itself. Forgiveness washes away each expression of evil and assures us of continued peace. But for true freedom

137

we must have release from the sinful nature's surging inner power.

PEACE AND POWER
Romans 6

In Romans 1—5, the apostle Paul has proclaimed the good news of peace with God. Christ's redemption, received by faith, offers forgiveness of sins.

Now, writing again in the distinctive form of the diatribe, in which the writer inserts periodic objections which an imaginary opponent may make, and then answers them, Paul raises an important question. What shall we conclude from this promise of forgiveness and peace? "Shall we go on sinning so that grace may increase" (6: 1)? Assured forgiveness might not only seem to be a license to sin; it might even be perverted to seem to be an invitation by God to keep on sinning so that His grace in forgiving might be enhanced!

Paul strikes back at this idea with an exclamation: "By no means!" (vs. 2). We might paraphrase it as an explosive "Heaven forbid!" "We died to sin," Paul insists; "how can we live in it any longer?"

What happened to the sin nature? Paul's explosion and the verses which immediately follow are the key to understanding the victory over sin which Christ has won for us.

Historically, there have been many different approaches to the "victorious Christian life." Each of them is related to a particular idea of what has happened to man's sin nature:

138

■ *Eradication.* According to this theory, when a person becomes a Christian the sin nature itself dies. This means that the very capacity to sin is removed; whatever a person desires or chooses must flow from the new in him and not the old. Our common experience and the Bible's assurance of *continued* forgiveness make it plain that this theory does not fit the facts.

■ *Suppression.* According to this theory, when a person becomes a Christian he is given the power to control his sin nature. The capacity and desire for sin is still present, but the Christian is responsible to hold down that desire.

In this approach a great deal of significance is placed on the Law as a tool for suppression. Guided by the Law's demands, and always aware of his own personal responsibility, the individual fights for mastery over his old self.

This grim struggle is something Paul describes in Romans 7. The apostle himself once took this route—and failed.

■ *Self-crucifixion.* Noting that we were crucified with Christ (see Rom. 6:6; Gal. 2:20), this approach to the Christian life visualizes our sin nature as something always struggling to get off the cross again. It is the believer's responsibility, then, to live the "crucified life." Each temptation calls for renewed surrender to God.

At times this approach to Christian living has led individuals to see every human desire and pleasure as an indication of sin. When this happens, they have been led into a joyless life of denying themselves

139

those very things which God gives us "richly . . . to enjoy" (I Tim. 6:17, KJV).

■ *Penalism.* This approach views all temptations as attacks of Satan. The problem is never located within us; it's always the fault of Satan. The response to Satan's attacks is to reject them, acting in the authority of Christ who at the cross won final victory over our enemy the devil.

The approach that Paul outlines in Romans 6 is different from each of the preceding four. His argument rests on a different understanding of what happened at the cross. And it teaches us a different way to respond to sin's inner pull, a way that promises us freedom and release such as we have never known.

This way of release is based on the understanding that through Christ's work on the cross our sin nature was rendered powerless. It still exists. It still exerts its pull. But we are no longer its slaves.

Romans 6:1-4. Paul begins here with the concept of identification or union with Christ. His point is that our union with Jesus is not only statutory but real. Because we are "in" Christ now, His death was our death, and His resurrection is our resurrection.

Being "in Christ" is the very root and essence of the new life of the Christian. We have passed from death to life (the powers of death have no hold on us anymore). We are not "in the flesh" or "in sin" anymore. It is as if we were in a new country—in Christ.

This being the case, we have a share in Christ's triumph over the forces of death and hell. As they could not hold Him in their power, they no longer hold us in their power. The cross, irradiated with the light of Easter morning, is now the fundamental fact which will determine not only our own personal history but the history of the cosmos as well.

Romans 6: 5-10. This crucifixion of the "old self" (a term for the sin nature) did not eradicate the old desires or motives. They continue to betray our "place of origin"—like a telltale accent that marks our speech. The crucifixion of the "old self" did not remove forever the pull of temptation. Instead, what happened was that the "body of sin" (that whole package of old and warped responses) was rendered powerless or inoperative (vs. 6). We will still feel the old temptations, *but we no longer are in their power.* Our days of slavery are ended. We are now free to choose the good.

Like Jesus, you and I are now alive to God, and we can choose to live for Him.

Romans 6:11-14. How is a believer to respond, then, when he feels the tug of sin? With faith!

We are to count ourselves dead to sin, but alive to God; and with full trust in the life of Jesus within us, we are to actively yield ourselves to God, turning over our whole selves to Him to use as instruments of righteousness.

The mastery of sin is finished.

The truths that Paul presents here in the early verses of Romans 6 do promise a victory and a freedom of which many of us have only dreamed. The practical implications of this teaching are astonishing.

The past is powerless. One of our greatest bondages

141

ROMANS 6:1-14

What Identification Means	*How We Respond to Find Victory*
I. Union with Christ in His death.	I. Understand what union with Jesus means.
Sin in our bodies is rendered inoperative, robbed of its lordship.	We were crucified with Christ that the dominance over the body of our sin nature might be rendered inoperative.
II. Union with Christ in His resurrection.	II. Believe (count what God says as true: "reckon").
We are made alive with Christ, free to serve God.	Stop turning yourself over to sin. Trust God's promise that you no longer must sin.
	III. Act on what you believe.
	Present yourselves to God rather than to sin and do His will.

has been to our past. In a very real way, what we have done has determined our future. The habits we've developed and the tastes we've cultivated have "programmed" our personalities. Each time we surrendered to a temptation, we made it harder to resist the next time. Each sin in which we indulged paved the way for the next.

But that whole cluster of programmed responses was dealt with on the cross! We still feel their pull, but our future choices are no longer determined by those decisions we made in the past. "I can't help myself" is no longer true!

We have so many ways to talk about the bondage we experienced in our past. "I can't stop myself" is a cry that expresses hopelessness. So is "The temptation is more than I can bear." No matter how true such statements may have been, they are no longer true. Now at last there is release and hope.

On God's own Word I am assured that the power of the past over my present has been broken by Jesus. I know that I can count on His promise. I choose to act, in faith, upon that Word.

Next time the conflict comes, I will present myself to God and let His righteousness find expression in me.

GOING DEEPER
to personalize

1. The author points out that peace with God is the possession of every believer through forgiveness. How far have you come in your own experience of forgiveness and peace? Draw an imaginary road map from Guilt City to the Place of Peace. Sketch in details, landmarks, crossroads, etc. Then mark (X) where you are on that journey.

2. Compare in a concordance the number of times

the Bible speaks about *forgiveness* and *guilt*. Then select one verse which seems to you to sum up the meaning of forgiveness.

3. Would you be satisfied if the Christian experience offered continuing forgiveness for sins but no hope for improving and changing your way of life? Why or why not?

4. Romans 6:1-14 is the basis for the victory teaching in Romans 6—8. Study it carefully, and then go on to read through the rest of this three-chapter section. Use the outline on page 122 to guide you.

5. *Baptism* is another word into which we tend to read preconceived meanings. To grasp its use in Romans 6, do the following:

(a) Write down every meaning of baptism that you know.

(b) Look up the following passages, and write down what baptism seems to refer to in each:

Matthew 3:11   I Corinthians 12:12, 13
Matthew 3:16   Acts 2:38-41

(c) Look at Romans 6:1-4 again. What baptism do you think this refers to, and why?

6. Romans 6:15-23 is a digression from Paul's main argument, answering the implied question, "If we are free from the Law (vs. 14), does this mean we are free to sin?" Read the passage carefully and see if you can sum up Paul's answer in no more than three sentences.

to probe

1. In a theology text, look up *identification* and *union with Christ*. What other passages in Scripture

144

contain this teaching?

2. On the basis of Romans 6, develop two lists of statements. One list should contain positive statements under this heading: What "freedom from sin" means. The other list should contain negative statements under the heading: What "freedom from sin" does not mean. Attempt to develop at least twelve of each type.

PEACE AND POWER

WE OFTEN THINK of Romans as a doctrinal book, full of deep and difficult truth. In fact, the Book of Romans is totally practical. In seeking to understand man's condition, Paul did not turn to abstract theory. Instead, he looked around him and saw in society and in each individual's experience the daily demonstration of the reality of sin.

In seeking to explain faith, Paul again resisted abstract philosophical argument. He went back to a historical situation and to a flesh-and-blood man, Abraham. He noted that, for Abraham, faith meant a very simple thing: unwavering trust in God's promise, the kind of trust that led Abraham to obey God.

Now, like the practical man he is, Paul turns his attention to how this new freedom from sin's power over us works. It's good to know that the sin in us has been rendered inoperative. But we still feel its pull! At times when we honestly want to respond to God, we may find ourselves actually choosing the opposite way. What does it take to live victoriously? How do we experience the divine power?

Paul's answer is simple, but so surprising that it demands explanation. "Sin will have no dominion over you, since you are not under law but under grace" (Rom. 6:14). Somehow the fact of our release from the Law to live the Christian life under grace is vital to our experience of freedom.

The argument. Chapters 7 and 8 hinge on the affirmation in 6:14 that believers are not under the Law but under grace. We can trace Paul's explanation by seeing each section as an answer to a question that flows from that statement, or as a digression from the main line of argument. These questions will help us think through this important passage with Paul.

Background. One additional concept of Paul's provides important background as we begin to think through this section of Romans.

Earlier we saw that the concept of spiritual death underlay Paul's teaching in Romans 1—3. There is another concept that underlies Paul's explanation in Romans 6—8 of the way to victory. This concept is that the believer has "two natures."

The Bible speaks very bluntly about our "sin nature," that tendency to sin which warps and distorts the human personality. Intended in the original Creation to reflect the character of God Himself (Gen. 1:26, 27), man's character was twisted out of its intended shape by the Fall. That warped and twisted nature, with its capacity and passion for

Line of Thought	Digression
NOT UNDER LAW, BUT UNDER GRACE (Rom. 6:14)	• Are we then free to sin? (6:15-23).
• *How* can we legally be freed from the Law? (7:1-3).	
• *Why* must we be freed from the Law? (7:4-6).	
	• If the Law is so closely related to sin, is the Law evil? (7:7-12).
• *What happens* to a believer who tries to relate to God through the Law? (7:13-25).	
• *What happens* to a believer who relates to God through the Holy Spirit? (8:1-8).	
• *What* is the source of our victory experience? (8:9-17).	

every way but God's way, remains with us.

But then God acted in Christ to effect His new creation! Those who believe are "made alive," and a new capacity for goodness is added which we never possessed before. With new life, each personality takes on a new dimension again. Now at last we have both the desire and the capacity to respond to God.

But we still retain the old nature as well! Within us the two capacities—the one for good and the other for evil—remain at war. And we ourselves—our reactions, motives, desires, values, and behavior— are the channels through which either God will express Himself and righteousness, or evil will find expression in sin.

The challenge of the Christian life is to learn to live as the new men which we are and to increasingly reject the old that we once were.

This distinctive understanding of the believer and his difference from all other men is basic to Paul's prescription for victory. Understanding this, let's

THE BELIEVER

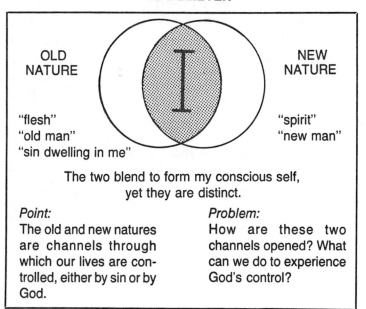

OLD NATURE

NEW NATURE

"flesh"
"old man"
"sin dwelling in me"

"spirit"
"new man"

The two blend to form my conscious self,
yet they are distinct.

Point:
The old and new natures are channels through which our lives are controlled, either by sin or by God.

Problem:
How are these two channels opened? What can we do to experience God's control?

149

examine, in order, the answers to the questions raised now by Paul.

ROMANS 7

How can we legally be free from the Law? (Rom. 7:1-3). Paul turns to marriage for an illustration. A married couple is bound to each other under the Law until one of them dies. The death of the partner frees *both* from the Law. Since our union with Christ is real, we also "died to the law through the body of Christ" (7:4).

Why must we be freed from the Law? (Rom. 7:4-6). This is an extremely significant question. It is, in fact, central to the Bible's whole teaching on the Law and the believer. Paul says that the old nature (our "sinful passions") is aroused (stimulated or energized) by the Law, with the result that we produce sin's deadly fruit. But now we are released from the Law and must relate to God in a new way. Now the Spirit speaks to us directly. And He energizes the new nature, with the result that we produce the fruit of righteousness.

TWO WAYS OF RELATING TO GOD

Through the Law	Through the Spirit
The Law energizes the old nature which produces fruit to death	The Spirit energizes the new nature which produces fruit of righteousness

We see this energizing principle at work everywhere. The child who is told, "Don't touch the cookies; they're for company," finds his hunger for a cookie increased. The forbidden seems far more desirable. When we approach life as interpreted through the Law, with everything marked off by do's and don'ts, the old nature is charged with energy. But when we approach life in God's new way, seeing each challenge as an opportunity to let God express Himself through us, we are on the way to victory.

What is the experience of the believer who places himself under the Law (7:13-25)? Paul again shows his practical bent. Looking back to his own experience after his conversion when as Saul he tried to live the Christian life under the Law, Paul shares the discouragement he felt. No matter how he tried, sin kept on expressing itself in him.

You and I have had the same experience. We've wanted to do good. We've tried to keep what we saw as good laws or rules, and we've known the shame and agony of failure. Paul's deeply personal words, paraphrased roughly here, share feelings we have known only too well!

I don't understand my own actions. I don't do what I want—I do the very thing I hate.

Because I don't want to do the things I do, it's clear that I agree that what the Law says is good and right. I'm in harmony with God that much. But somehow I'm not in control of my own actions! Some sinful force within takes over and acts through my body.

I know that nothing good exists in the old me. The

151

sin nature is so warped that even when I desire good I somehow can't do it. Sin, dwelling in me, is to blame for this situation.

It all seems hopeless! The fact is that when I want to do right, evil lies close at hand. In my inmost self I delight in God's law. But another principle wars with the desire to obey and brings me as a captive to my knees before the principle of indwelling sin.

Paul's effort to keep the Law, with which he agrees, has failed. The sin nature has retained enough control over him to make it plain that he falls far short of the holiness and goodness he desires.

ROMANS 8

Romans 7 ends with a cry: "What a wretched man I am! Who will rescue me from this body of death?" (vs. 24).

Romans 8:1, 2 answers: "There is now no condemnation . . . because through Christ Jesus the law of the Spirit of life set me free from the law of sin and death." Sin within is overcome by a new principle, that of the "Spirit of life." Simply put, Paul finds his answer in realizing that he cannot keep the Law . . . and in no longer trying! Paul no longer feels any obligation to try. He accepts himself as *really* being a sinner with no hope of pleasing God or doing good. Even as a Christian, he now goes back to the cross and finds joy in the thought of "no condemnation."

Then Paul makes the great discovery! When he stops *trying* and instead relies on God to express His life through him, then "the righteous requirements

COMPARISON: ROMANS 7 and 8

Chapter 7	Chapter 8
I struggle to keep the Law.	I yield myself to Jesus.
Battlefield: self-effort	*Battlefield:* enablement
Combatants: law of sin in the flesh vs. law of the mind	*Combatants:* law of sin in the flesh vs. Spirit of life in Christ Jesus
Outcome: I serve sin.	*Outcome:* The requirements of the Law are fulfilled in us.
Summary: Romans 7: 4-6	*Summary:* Romans 8: 8-11
NOTE Relating to God through an impersonal code: "law"—20 times "I"—22 times "I do"—14 times	NOTE Relating to God personally through faith: "law"—4 times "Holy Spirit"—20 times

of the law" are "fully met" in him (vs. 4)! Sin lives in Paul, but Christ lives within him too! If Paul does not concentrate on keeping the Law but on trusting Jesus, the Spirit will energize the new nature, resulting in a righteous life.

Our obligation, then, is not to the Law, but to respond to the leading of the Holy Spirit (vss. 12,

14). The pedagogue has been replaced by a personal relationship with God. That relationship is so intimate and real that we come to Him with the delighted infant cry, "Abba" (meaning "Daddy!").

In the Christian life, if we focus on the Law and on right or wrong actions as our goal, we will invariably miss the point of our great adventure. *The Christian is called into a personal relationship with God!* It is the closeness of our relationship with Him that is to be the focus of our attention and the center of our desire. This relationship is real. We are now God's children. Christ is in us; His Spirit is present. Deepening our relationship with this wonderful Person who has sought us out is the whole duty of the believer, and it is the key to victory.

How can a relationship be the key to victory? How does a relationship produce righteousness? Paul's answer is that as we deepen our relationship with God, the Spirit of God gains more and more control over our lives. Then the Spirit will "give life to your mortal bodies" (vs. 11) even though they are dead because of indwelling sin. It takes resurrection, life from the dead, for a human being to live a righteous life. And resurrection is exactly what God provides for those who "live in accordance with the Spirit and have their minds set on what the Spirit desires" (vs. 5).

Romans 8:18-30. In Romans 5, Paul concluded his explanation of the Gospel by stating an underlying principle: All men are spiritually dead; they desperately need righteousness and can only receive it as a gift.

154

Now, in Romans 8, as Paul concludes his explanation of how the Gospel can produce righteousness in a believer, he again states a principle underlying the whole argument. God has chosen to shape redeemed men in the likeness of His Son Jesus. It is our destiny to be like Christ. God is committed to produce in us all the love, all the joy, all the patience, all the longsuffering, all the goodness, and all the gentleness of Jesus.

This commitment means ultimately the renewal and transformation of the whole creation. It means that one day sin will be eradicated and that we will be "brought into the glorious freedom of the children of God" (vs. 18). It also means that *now* we have hope. In another passage, Paul speaks of a progressive transformation, of a *growth* in Christlikeness which we can expect to take place. "We . . . are being transformed into his likeness," Paul writes the Corinthians, "with ever-increasing glory, which comes from the Lord, who is the Spirit" (II Cor. 3:18). As the Spirit of God shapes the likeness of Jesus within us, we need never concern ourselves with the Law. The life of Jesus will overflow in spontaneous righteousness.

What the Law could never produce, the Spirit of God within us *is* now producing.

THE NEW TESTAMENT ON THE LAW

At this point, then, we can summarize the New Testament teaching on the Law and see it in a clearer perspective.

155

The Law itself is "holy, and the commandment is holy, righteous and good" (Rom. 7:12). As such, the Law has several important characteristics:

■ It reveals the moral character of God as holy and good.

■ It establishes standards by which persons can measure and evaluate behavior.

■ It provides a partial explanation of righteousness, illustrating righteous behavior and specifying what is unrighteous.

The Law (defined in this context as the moral and social commands given to Israel) is definitely *revelational;* it is designed to help us know more about both God and what is good. The Law's revelation of what is holy is taught in Scripture to have several definite functions. These functions, strikingly, relate to the "old man" or the "sin nature"!

■ The Law is designed to bring the knowledge of sin. When a person looks at the Law's demands and then reflects upon his own deeds, he becomes aware that he is a sinner.

■ The Law is designed to stir up sin in us. This overlooked function is one often mentioned in the Bible. "The law was added so that the trespass might increase," Paul says (Rom. 5:20). "When the commandment came, sin sprang to life" (7:9). Because man *is* a rebel, God's commands stimulate his rebelliousness.

■ The Law is designed to demonstrate man's need for Christ. Only a person who has given up and ceased to rely on his own efforts is likely to be ready to turn to faith. Our natural tendency is to "try harder." If we look honestly at our lives in the Law's light, we see how futile such self-effort is.

The Law and the believer. In theology it's common to distinguish three functions of the Law: (1) to reveal God, (2) to convict of sin, and (3) to guide the believer's response to God. This third function is one over which there has been conflict. Some say that during the Old Testament era believers were guided to respond to God through the Law, but the New Testament era introduced the new faith principle of which Paul speaks in Romans 8. Others say that the Christian is expected to keep the Law today and that the Law is still the way God guides us to please Him. Neither of these notions seems to fit the biblical facts.

The point made in Romans is that the Law *always* relates to the old nature (the capacity for sin in man). What's more, the Law always *energizes* that sin nature. This is true whether a person is spiritually dead (and possesses only one nature) or is spiritually alive (and possesses the two natures—the sin capacity and the new life capacity). The Law has *never* been the way that believers related to God. Always the true believer, both in Old and New Testament times, responded to God as a person. Even when listening to the pedagogue and being subject to its guardianship, the true believer heard through the Law the loving voice of God and was freed to respond only by faith in Him.

The Old Testament principle of life by faith (presented by Paul in Romans 4) was missed by Israel. They distorted the Law into something it had never

157

been meant to be. They tried to make it a way of salvation. They tried to make it a ladder on which to climb, rung by rung, to claim a place beside God as good. In so doing, they lost sight of God Himself, ignored a personal relationship with Him, and thus fell from grace.

And so can we.

We too can read about righteousness in the Scripture, and take its teachings as rules and laws to live by. We can make the mistake of seeing God as a rule maker, and the Bible as a rule book for the game of life. Throwing our energies into vigorous attempts to fulfill the "oughts" and "shoulds," we take our eyes off the Lord and our personal relationship with Him. We miss the growing closeness to Jesus to which we are called. We miss the daily, warm, loving guidance of the Spirit. We miss the freedom to rush to God and call the Father "Daddy."

When we try to live by the Law, the joy of adventure is lost, and the inward battle with sin wears away our hope.

How different is God's way!

What a thrill to realize that God accepts us as we are: imperfect, falling short of goodness, and yet, because Christ *is* in us, growing toward His likeness. For our present sins and failures we have forgiveness. "There is now no condemnation for those who are in Christ Jesus" (Rom. 8: 1). For the rest of our life we have the promise of progress toward God's great goal for us: being made in the likeness of Jesus. As we grow in Him, His life will overflow. "The life I now live in the body, I live by faith in the Son of God" is how Paul put it in Galatians 2:20. As His life surges up within me, all the righteousness which the Law ever envisioned, and even more, will find its expression in me.

In Jesus there is peace—and power!

GOING DEEPER
to personalize

1. Study carefully Romans 7:1—8:17, guided by the charts and outlines in this chapter. As you study, make two separate lists: "Things I understand" and "Things I don't understand."

2. Without looking back over the chapter, explain in your own words each of the following:

(a) the believer's two natures

(b) the relationship between the Law and the old nature

(c) the experience of the believer under the Law

3. In I Corinthians 15:56 Paul makes an enigmatic statement: "The sting of death is sin, and the power of sin is the law." On the basis of Romans 6—8, how would you explain this statement?

4. Often abstract ideas become more clear when we use analogies and illustrations. For example, it helps if we picture the Law as:

(a) a mirror which shows us ourselves as sinners

(b) a magnet which pulls at the sin nature within us

(c) *not* a ladder, for it was not meant for us to climb on

How many other analogies suggest themselves to you as you think through this passage of Scripture and the text discussion?

5. Paul ends Romans 8 with a great shout of praise and joy. Read verses 31-39 carefully, and write a verse-by-verse commentary on them. Relate each thought to what Paul has been saying in chapters 6—8 on how God works to produce righteousness now that we are freed from the Law.

to probe

1. Do a careful comparison of what Galatians and Romans teach about the Law. (Note particularly where a concept in one explains or expands a concept stated in the other.) Write at least five to eight pages.

2. Do a careful comparison of what Galatians and Romans teach about the Christian life. (Note particularly where a concept in one explains or expands a concept stated in the other.) Again, write five to eight pages.

3. Do a careful analysis of your own Christian experience. How much of it has been lived in Romans 7? How much of it has been lived in Romans 8? Have you learned anything that might help others grow as Christians or understand the distinctive "by faith" life-style?

TIME ENOUGH

"BUT I WANT to be able to draw like Paul *now!*"
Every so often our youngest, Tim, is filled with an
awful sense of urgency. He feels a terrible need at
thirteen to be able to do everything his nineteen-
year-old brother does. And to do it just as well.

We hear it on the basketball court when Tim miss-
es. We hear it at times when the two boys sit down
together. *Now* is a burden for Tim in many ways. He
knows so many things that he'll be able to do only in
the future.

I can understand Tim's feelings. You can too.
Often we feel the same kind of urgency to see more
evidence of Christ's presence in our lives. We want
to be like Jesus *now.* The dimensions in which we still
need to grow bother us deeply. We feel like the
apostle Paul when he placed himself under the Law
and struggled to live up to the righteousness he saw
expressed there. He tried. And when he failed, he
felt condemned.

But then God taught him those truths which he

shares with us in Galatians and Romans.

God has taken us out from under the Law. It did its work in making us aware of our sin and failure. The Law did its work in making us feel condemned. The Law did its work in forcing us to look away from ourselves to God—to find some other way.

God had that other way prepared. Righteousness is imputed to men through faith. The death of Christ provides a basis on which forgiveness can be extended, freely, to all. What's more, this faith through which forgiveness comes also provides a way to actually become righteous. Through faith, in a deepening personal relationship with God, the new in us grows, and the Spirit's power is released to shape Christ Himself in our personalities.

The *Law* shouted out demands, telling us what we should be but are not.

Grace invites us to accept ourselves as forgiven men and women now and to trust God to help us become.

The *becoming* takes time. The becoming sometimes disturbs us. We fail to see that God seeks progress rather than perfection. When we step out from under the Law and realize that we have been given time enough to grow, the pressure is removed, and we find a new freedom and joy. We can be ourselves—as immature and unskilled in God's ways as Tim is in his games—and yet rejoice in the fact that we still please God. We are growing, and His love is eternally ours.

He does not condemn.

Nothing can separate us from the love of Christ.

Paul's words of praise in Romans 8 brought out-raged objection from the Jews. If God is so steadfast in His love, why has He abandoned Israel? Why have the promises to God's Old Testament people been so summarily set aside to the benefit of Gentiles? Can Paul's God of righteousness justify His behavior toward the Jews?

On the surface, the Israelites had a strong case. We cannot read the Old Testament without being struck by the fact that God outlines there a glorious future for the Jews. They, the descendants of Abraham, are promised the land of Palestine as a perpetual possession. They, the descendants of Abraham, are promised a special relationship with God in which He claims them as His own. They, the people of David, are promised that one day a descendant of David will mount his throne and rule not only over Israel but over the entire earth as well.

When this promised King, the Messiah, comes, then Israel is to enter her days of glory. Israel's God will be recognized by all. The Gentiles will come to the Jews to learn of God and will recognize the Lord as Lord of all. In those days of glory, peace will cover the whole earth, and the Messiah-King will enforce righteousness. Thus, the blessing of all mankind depends on the Jew. The proud, despising Gentile will recognize that Israel has been right all along.

All this was Israel's heritage. All this was Israel's hope.

When Jesus came, everything seemed to change.

163

The One whom Paul proclaimed as Messiah and Lord rejected a throne and chose a cross instead. Now Paul was preaching Jesus and faith to the Gentiles. The promise of the coming Kingdom seemed set aside, and Paul spoke instead of righteousness. Becoming like Jesus, not ruling with the King, became the focal point of the great missionary's concern. All of Israel's dreams of glory seemed shattered. Had God's Word and promise been broken? How could Paul dare to speak of such a faithless God as being righteous? How could Paul write of confidence in such a God's enduring love?

God's answer is given in these next chapters of Romans. We can understand the present only when we see it in the perspective of what God has done in the past and what He will do in the future.

This is important for our Tim—and for you and me. When we sense the gap between what we are and what we yearn to be, we need to look back and to look ahead to what we will be when God is finished with us: persons who reflect fully all that Jesus is in His righteousness. We are *in the process* of moving toward that goal, and we cannot really know ourselves or God's grace until we see our lives in the perspective of the whole of God's great plan for us.

It's the same with God's dealings with Israel. The Jewish objectors failed to see the righteousness of God's actions. They lacked perspective and failed to understand either past history or history to come. Looking at history now, Paul introduces us to a God who is both righteous and sovereign.

164

ISRAEL'S REJECTION
Romans 9:1-33

Paul is proud of his Hebrew heritage. He feels deep sorrow and anguish for those of his race who have not responded with faith in their Messiah. As God's chosen, they have enjoyed many honors and privileges: the Covenant, the promises, the patriarchs, even the privilege of being the human line through whom Christ was born.

The failure of Israel to respond is not, however, a failure of the Word of God. God's Word and His purposes will never fail. This is a fact which Israel's own history demonstrates.

Romans 9:7-13. In the first place, the promises to Israel never were intended to include *all* physical descendants of Abraham. Ishmael, even though a child of Abraham, was not in the line of Covenant promise; only Isaac was (Gen. 21:12). Even in the case of twin sons of the same parents, God's purpose included one and not the other. Before the boys were even born (and thus before they had done either good or bad), God announced that one was chosen and the other rejected.

Hated. The phrase "Esau I hated" (vs. 13) reflects an ancient inheritance formula. God chose Jacob as heir to the promise and decisively rejected Esau.

It's clear that God's promise, the word he spoke to Israel, never did include *all* Israelites.

Romans 9:14-24. But isn't this choice of some and not others unfair? The idea that God actually chooses some to receive His gifts and grace and does

165

not choose others has been hard for many to accept. Paul's answer is to insist that God's mercy "does not . . . depend on man's desire or effort, but on God's mercy" (vs. 16). God acts freely and sovereignly. He is God, and no man has a right to question His actions.

It is not, of course, that God forces evil people (like Pharaoh) to do evil against their will. In fact, God's goodness itself hardens the evil ones. In their deadness, they choose to reject Him (see Rom. 1). Paul's point is that God is not *obligated* to show mercy on anyone. Yet in mercy He does choose to show both His goodness and His wrath.

Romans 9:22-33. The New Testament revelation of God's grace in Jesus may surprise the Jews by its inclusion of Gentiles. But it should not. Not only did the Old Testament foretell that one day God would welcome others as "my people," but it also made it plain that not all Israelites are counted by God as His own. "Though the number of the Israelites should be like the sand of the sea," Isaiah has prophesied, "only the remnant will be saved" (vs. 27).

Paul concludes that Israel's present experience is in full harmony with the way God has acted and spoken in the past. There has been no failure of God's Word; it remains fully trustworthy. The failure has been in Israel herself, in chasing after righteousness as though it were to be gained by works. The Gentiles—ignorant of righteousness—have found it now, by faith.

ISRAEL'S REJECTION EXPLAINED
Romans 10

Romans 10:1-4. Paul again shares his own deep desire for the Israelites to be saved. He says it again: "They disregarded the righteousness that comes from God and sought to establish their own, they did not submit to God's righteousness" (vs. 3). Because Israel was unwilling to approach God on the basis of faith and instead insisted on misusing the Law as an avenue of approach, the nation's rejection is deserved.

Romans 10:5-11. Christ has come down from heaven, died, and risen again. All that is left for man to do is believe. Faith now puts the Gentile on a par with the Jew. God is God to all, and He blesses each person who calls on Him.

Romans 10:14-18. The universality of the Gospel impels its proclamation. The explosive missionary ministry of the Church reflects the very nature of the Word itself. Even though that good news was spoken to Israel in the past, it brought no universal faith. Though all had heard, not all had believed.

Romans 10:19-21. It follows that proclamation of the Gospel to the Gentiles is not evidence of God's rejection of the Jews. Instead, it is evidence of the Jews' rejection of God! God has spoken to all men. Perhaps the Gentile response will move a disobedient and obstinate Israel to envy, and, awakened by anger, some may hear.

167

REJECTION INCOMPLETE
Romans 11

A remnant (Rom. 11:1-10). Israel's present situation, while deserved, is hardly complete rejection. Paul himself is a Jew, and yet he is a believer. The early church for its first decade was a Hebrew church. As in Old Testament times, God has reserved a remnant of Israel to be His own. There are *thousands* of Jewish believers. As always, a remnant has been chosen—by grace.

A restoration (Rom. 11:11-36). Looking now at the great mass of Israel, Paul asks if their fall is beyond recovery. His answer is a resounding no. Israel has been temporarily set aside and the stream of faith diverted to enrich the Gentile world. But restoration will come—and with it even greater riches for all mankind.

In the meantime there is no cause for those who now experience God's kindness to boast. Israel remains chosen. Her dead branches, broken off because of unbelief, made room for us who are now nourished on Israel's vine. We stand in grace, not by any innate right, but only by faith. And God surely is able to graft restored Israel back into her own vine.

Speaking now to Gentiles, Paul states that such a regrafting is exactly God's intention. When "the full number of the Gentiles" has come in, "all Israel will be saved" (11:25, 26). The Deliverer, Jesus, will come from Zion. The people of Jacob (the Israelites) will be turned to God and know forgiveness. All that God has promised them will surely come to pass.

"God's gifts and his call are irrevocable" (11:29).

Paul's concluding doxology of praise (11:33-36) has a vital message for Israel and for us today:

> Oh, the depth of the riches, the wisdom and the
> knowledge of God!
> How unsearchable his judgments,
> and his paths beyond tracing out!
> Who has known the mind of the Lord?
> Or who has been his adviser?
> Who has ever given to God,
> that God should repay him?
> For from him and through him and to him are all
> things.
> To him be the glory forever! Amen.

Paul, glimpsing the vastness and complexity of God's purpose in history, lifts his voice and bows his head in praise. The Jew who accused God of unfaithfulness to His Word erred in underestimating God. He had only a superficial view of God's plan and purpose. Rather than submit to God and seek to understand the whole, he actually dared condemn the Lord of all!

How often we're tempted to do the same.

■ We bridle at Paul's blunt statement of God's sovereignty and its expression in His choice of some to receive mercy (Rom. 9). We can't understand how this fits in with the revelation in Jesus of a God of love who is unwilling that *any* should perish (II Pet. 3:9). Instead of trusting God's wisdom, righteousness, and love, we, like the unbelieving Jew of Paul's day, cry out, "Unfair!"

169

So what if we cannot understand? Is God accountable to us? Is our sense of justice more acute than His? Or can we, like Paul, see such things that are beyond our comprehension as fresh evidence of the depth of the wisdom and knowledge of God? A wisdom and knowledge we cannot plumb—but a wisdom to which we *can* surrender in trust.

■ We complain and grumble about the slowness of our growth. Why the ups and downs? Why do some of our problems persist so long? "Am I really profiting from these years of bouts with depression? Why has God put off healing the hurts which divide my home?"

Yet Scripture demands that we see everything happening in our lives as an element in God's good plan for our growth and glorification. "In all things God works for the good of those who love him" (Rom. 8: 28), Paul affirms. We have been called "according to his purpose" (vs. 28b), and our lives are designed so that purpose of forming Christ in us might proceed at God's carefully designed pace.

Looking at the pattern of my life, I must be willing to surrender my perspective to Him. He is the Lord; I am not His adviser. His wisdom is beyond my own, and I surrender in praise to that wisdom.

■ We fear to step out into freedom, even when we hear His word, "You are not under law, but under grace" (Rom. 6: 14). Can *faith* make me righteous? Is it safe to abandon the safety of the Law's bars to prowl outside? Can the Holy Spirit within really keep the tiger tamed?

How tragic when we underestimate God. How

tragic when we, like the ancient Jew, fail to read the lesson of history past and history to come. God's wisdom *is* far beyond anything we can understand or grasp. *But what God says is true.* With complete confidence in the wisdom of God, I can bow before Him and surrender my wisdom to His.

From this day forward I can live.

By faith.

And to experience in a life focused totally in Jesus the greatest adventure of all.

> For from him and through him and to him are all things.
> To him be the glory forever! Amen.
> *Romans 11:36*

GOING DEEPER
to personalize

1. The author suggests that historical perspective is vital for us in seeing both the righteousness of God in our individual experience and in His dealing with Israel.

(a) Draw a time line, showing your own history and destiny. Mark your conversion, where you are now, any important changes or growth along the way, and where it will be in the future.

(b) Remembering God's purpose of shaping Christ in us (Rom. 8:29; Gal. 5:22, 23), indicate along the time line any significant changes toward Christlikeness that have taken place.

(c) Also explore this question: How does God in-

tend to use this present Bible study in your growth process? What have you learned that will help accelerate your growth? How are you going to use what you've been learning (or how are you using it)?

2. Read Romans 9 through 11 carefully, guided by the outline and brief notes in the text. Jot down anything that is hard for you to understand or to accept.

3. Read as your own prayer and confession of faith the doxology with which Paul ends Romans 11. Can you abandon your own wisdom and understanding to God's? Can you trust God for what you cannot explain?

How good to know that God is the kind of person we can love and trust. If we did not know Him, it would be really difficult to do.

to probe

1. Prepare for a final test over these chapters in Acts and over James, Galatians, and Romans. Jot down the main topics and issues covered, and be sure you know the historical setting in which each epistle took shape.

2. Do a study of the Bible's teaching about God's sovereignty. Title your paper, "How knowing God in Jesus affects my understanding of God's sovereignty." Use not only Romans but also any additional Old or New Testament Scriptures you wish.

THE GREAT ADVENTURE BEGINS

Date (approx.)	Scripture	
33	Acts 1—3	The Church begins
34	Acts 4	*Homothumadon:* unity and community
34—44	James	Faith's life-style in the early Hebrew church
40—44	Acts 5—9	Persecution and early expansion in Judea, Samaria
44—46	Acts 10—11	First Gentile converts
46—48	Acts 12—14	Paul's first missionary journey
48	Acts 15	Jerusalem Council confirms: Gentile Christians not under the Law
49	Galatians	Relationship between the Law and the Gospel 1. The Law is not involved in salvation past or present (Gal. 1—4). 2. The Holy Spirit works through new life (Gal. 5, 6).
55*	Romans	The revelation of God's righteousness apart from the Law 1. *Deliverance:* All men are dead in sin and need righteousness provided (Rom. 1—5). 2. *Victory:* Christ provides power to live a righteous life now (Rom. 6—8). 3. *History:* God's righteous plan is being worked out in the past, present, and future (Rom. 9—11). 4. *Community:* God's righteousness finds unique expression in a loving community (Rom. 12—16).

*NOTE: Romans is studied out of its time sequence because its theme is so closely related to that of Galatians and to the critical question of the early church: the relationship between the Law and faith, new life and righteousness.

173

WITH ONE VOICE

I DON'T KNOW why we picture righteous people as dull.

But we do.

And we picture them as somehow rather grim. As standing to one side, with a disapproving look on their faces while others frolic. Somehow the righteous person shows up dressed in black while everyone else wears bright and colorful clothes. In the old movies we watch on TV, the scoundrel is the warm, engaging person who makes friends.

How tragic when we let the world force our thinking into Satan's mold. Righteousness isn't like that at all! The righteousness that God gives us, and the righteousness that His Spirit is at work to shape in us, is a warmly personal kind of thing. Rather than isolate us from others, for the first time we find it's possible to draw truly near. We find that the first fruit of the Spirit, love, warms and deepens our relationships with others who have become our brothers and sisters, one with us in the forever family of God. The second product, joy, makes the fellowship we share bright and colorful.

So let's exchange our old mistaken picture of righteousness for reality. Let's take off our imaginary suits of black. Let's put on our brightest party clothes. Let's reach out to others . . . stretch out our hands . . . touch . . . smile. Let's call for the music to play, the celebration to begin! Let's move out into the sunlight, feel its warmth, shout together, share our joy!

The righteousness of God finds fullest expression in Christ's new and loving community.

Homothumadon. Perhaps you remember that Greek word meaning "with one accord" from our earlier study in Acts. It was a word that God chose to describe the fellowship of the earliest church. It was this unique dimension of harmony and love that so surprised the early observers. "See how they love one another" was the remark. These people, so varied in background (there were both rich and poor), found a unity and love that observers could hardly believe.

Jesus had spoken of this dimension of Christian community before His crucifixion: "Love one another . . . as I have loved you." He told His followers, "By this all men will know that you are my disciples, if you have love for one another" (Jn. 13: 34, 35). God's plan for believers includes the demonstration of His righteousness in and through a loving community. Christ's church is to demonstrate to all the world that righteousness, correctly

175

understood, means love and joy!

The church is also to be the context in which growth and transformation take place in believers. We are to be nourished in our growth toward Christ's likeness by one another. In the acceptance and love of our brothers and sisters, we're to sense God's own acceptance and love, and grow in that freedom from the Law which Paul has explained so carefully. "Growing up into Christ," Paul calls it in talking about this same thing in Ephesians 4:15. Growing up, together, into Christ.

It is tragic that just as the Law has sometimes been distorted and misused by Christians, the church has too. Sometimes, rather than the joyful community of God's plan, the church has become a joyless assembly. Rather than loving and accepting one another as brothers sharing a common pilgrimage, some churches have become legalistic assemblies where conformity and pretense are the price of admission. The vital dimension of growth in Christ as a way of life has been set aside, and agreement on our doctrines or convictions and customs has been imposed. No longer are imperfect people welcomed, loved, and accepted as they are in the calm assurance that growth in Christ is all they need. Instead, the believer is forced to try to hide his imperfections and struggle to live up to a new legalism imposed not by God but by men.

No wonder then that Paul, all too familiar with this same tendency in his own day, turns in the closing chapters of Romans to sketch for us the righteous community that God is shaping. He gives us clear and simple guidance for the shared experience of God's joy.

CHRIST'S IMPACT
Romans 12, 13

Romans 12 begins with familiar and famous words. "I urge you, . . . in view of God's mercy, to offer yourselves as living sacrifices, holy and pleasing to God—which is your spiritual worship."

Our bodies are to be surrendered to God for His righteous use (Rom. 6). In God's hand, the whole pattern of our lives will be transformed. We will no longer fit into the mold of this world and its ways, but with increasing insight into the divine perspective, our whole outlook and experience will change.

All too often this exhortation is treated as an isolated thing. Its connection with the context of chapters 12 and 13 is missed. In fact, Paul moves directly from this initial statement to explain the interpersonal impact of God's transformation.

Not alone (Rom. 12:3-8). The world's way of looking at people is in terms of their competitive capacity. We are judged *against* others.

This competitive dimension of society shows up in everything. School grades are a way of measuring persons against others. Sports are designed to select winners and separate them from losers. Our economy and business are again expressions of a competitive approach to life. The way we look at others and our opinion of them are directly related to how they compare in terms of skills, education, looks, talents, character traits, etc. In tremendously significant ways, each individual stands or falls alone.

And then we come to Christ . . . and our perspective is transformed. God thinks of us as members of a body. We do not compete in this body relationship; we cooperate! Each of us has a different function, but this difference doesn't make us better or worse than our brothers and sisters. It simply means that when we evaluate ourselves, we now use a new and sober kind of judgment. We find fulfillment is using the particular gift we have in concert with others. And we appreciate others for what they contribute to us. Each gift is important; each person has his or her own contribution to make.

No longer am I any more important than my brother. We are each important to the whole.

It is impossible to overestimate the practical impact of this new perspective which transformation will bring.
- Fulfillment for me without jealousy
- Relationships with others that are not distorted by status, for each of us is equally important to the whole
- Appreciation by others for who I am, not for my superior accomplishments
- A whole new way of relating to other people that is unlike anything the world knows.

In all of these ways and others, transformation affects my relationships in Christ's new community and frees the church to become His righteous family, marked by love.

Love (Rom. 12:9-21). The actuating power for life in God's new community is love. Paul makes this very clear. "Love must be sincere. Be devoted to one another in brotherly love. Live in harmony with one another. Overcome evil with good" (vss. 9, 10, 16, 21).

The kind of love that Paul describes is not a passive thing. Instead, it involves an aggressive reaching out to care for others. "Share with God's people who are in need" (vs. 13) is one practical way of reaching out in love. "Practice hospitality" (vs. 13) is another. "Be willing to associate with people of low position" (vs. 16) is yet another.

A climate of love is absolutely basic to the church of Jesus Christ. Without this attitude of caring and reaching out to touch one another's lives, the church will fall tragically short of God's intended experience for us of His "good, pleasing and perfect will" (12:2).

The major interpersonal implications of transformation are focused throughout Scripture on relationships between brothers and sisters in Christ's Body. But there are also implications for us as we live our lives in society. While human society operates on principles very different from those of God's new community, Christians are to live righteously within their society and culture.

The state (Rom. 13:1-7). Paul teaches that God has instituted human government as a restraining power, an agent of justice to bring punishment to the wrongdoer. This is not a blanket endorsement of every form of human government or of governmen-

179

tal systems. Even the best of governments fall short of the ideal. Still the Christian gives respect to the government under which he lives. In human society, government still represents God's concern for justice, and it is right for believers to submit.

Corrupt society (Rom. 13:8-14). The Christian is commanded by God to submit to human government. Is the believer to adopt all the ways of the society or culture in which he lives? Of course not! Our obligation to our fellowman is to love. So all those dark ways of men which run counter to love are to be "put aside" (13:12) by us. Clothed with the Lord Jesus, believers live as He Himself would live, as lights in the darkness of a world that is lost.

MAINTAINING HARMONY
Romans 14:1–15:13

Paul's primary concern, and God's, is not how the Christian conducts himself in society but how he expresses his new life within the believing community.

This isn't because life in society is unimportant. It is *because the community witnesses to the reality of Jesus* as well as does the individual. It is *only within the community* that individuals can grow to their full stature as Christ's people. The testimony to the reality of God and the nature of His righteousness depends significantly on the church truly *being* that righteous, loving community of *homothumadon.*

No wonder, then, that Paul turns to describe the attitudes toward others that we need to cultivate to build community. Strikingly, each of the attitudes discussed reflects significantly God's own attitude toward *us!*

Uncondemned (Rom. 14:1-13). How often a young Christian comes into contact with other believers—only to be condemned by them. "Why, he still *smokes!*" is something I used to hear of others. "He believes false doctrine! Why, he actually believes that a person who has been saved can be lost." I've heard that too. And many other things—criticisms against brothers who differ from us in ways that we somehow feel are very important.

Paul has a vital word for us. "Accept him whose faith is weak, without passing judgment on disputable matters" (14:1). For once and for always, surrender your "right" to judge and condemn another person who is, like you, a servant of God.

Paul is very blunt here. Christ died and rose again so that *He* might be the Lord. You didn't. No one proclaimed *you* God. Then, how dare you play God and judge your brother or look down on him? Scripture even says, "Who is he that condemns?" and answers that Christ Himself does not *condemn.* Rather, He is "interceding for us" (Rom. 8:34).

God's attitude toward the believer who has a long way to grow is one of acceptance and love. God has committed Himself to the person who has trusted Jesus, and "he will stand, for the Lord is able to make him stand" (14:4).

It is very important within the Christian community, then, that we look at others as well as ourselves in the framework of process. Whatever a brother

181

might be now, God is at work in his life. Because of Christ's presence, God will make that brother stand. Since God takes the long view and sees the individual in terms of his past and his destiny as well as his present, we must too. We also must accept, not condemn, and trust God to use acceptance and love in each of our lives for growth.

Self-sacrificing (Rom. 14:13–15:4). Often differences will concern Christians and trouble the entire fellowship. Some who have "freedom" may by exercising their freedom move a brother whose conscience isn't clear to imitate them, or they may encourage judging and critical attitudes.

There's no question that the Christian has a right to his freedom. But Paul suggests that another concern has priority. The Kingdom of God is a matter of "righteousness, peace and joy in the Holy Spirit" (14:17). The community—its peace and functioning as a loving family—is more important because *people* are more important.

What this means in practice is that "acting in love" (14:15) becomes more important to us than insisting on our rights. When it comes to a choice between loving concern for a brother and maintaining the correctness of our view of the privilege of certain practices, we choose love every time. "Even Christ did not please himself" (15:3), Paul reminds us. His example teaches us how to live with our brothers in order that God's goal of unity in the Body of Christ might be attained.

The goal (Rom. 15:5-13). That goal of unity is an exciting one for all of us. How enthusiastically Paul outlines it. How happily he invites us to experience the newness of our relationship with others.

> May the God of hope fill you with great joy and peace as you trust in him, so that you may overflow with hope by the power of the Holy Spirit.
>
> *Romans 15:13*

Adopting God's perspective and experiencing the new community, life's adventure promises just such overflowing joy.

FAREWELLS
Romans 15:14–16:27

Paul's farewells are revealing. He expresses confidence in the Spirit who is with the Romans. They do not need him, for they themselves have been fully equipped by God for their new life's great adventure (15:14-16).

While Paul has long wished to visit Rome, God has not yet let him. Eagerly he looks forward to such a time, perhaps as a side visit on the way to Spain. What an adventure there: Spain! A land where the Gospel has not yet been heard.

Chapter 16 is filled with personal greetings. If ever we wondered about the apostle and his relationships with others, these greetings are revealing. Paul has never visited Rome. He must have met these people elsewhere on his journeys. Yet, he's kept such close track that he knows the details of many of their lives. What a warm and loving relationship Paul must have found with his beloved brothers and sisters in the Lord. How real the community of which he writes must have been to him. Saul, the lonely Pharisee of thirty, isolated from everyone in that distorted righteousness of works, has become Paul the apostle, a man of warmth and love wrapped in the comforting cloak of Christian friends. God's kind of righteousness has broken through the isolation of the lonely heart and, in the fellowship of those who love one Lord, brought celebration and joy.

Look at the listed names:

With Paul:	At Rome:		Women
	Men		*Women*
Timothy	Aquila	Rufus	Priscilla
Lucius	Epaenetus	Asyncritus	Mary
Jason	Andronicus	Phlegon	Tryphena
Sosipater	Ampliatus	Hermes	Tryphosa
Tertius	Urbanus	Patrobas	Persis
Gaius	Stachys	Hermas	Julia
Erastus	Herodion	Nereus	
Quartus	Olympas	Junias	
Phoebe	Apelles	Philologus	

In Christ, community is ours.

Yet, our names are known individually.

Our individuality is not lost. In the new life of faith, we can at last become all we're meant to be.

184

GOING DEEPER
to personalize

1. Read through Romans 12—16 carefully, writing down every word that speaks of or characterizes personal relationships with the Body of Christ.

2. Many have debated the implications of Romans 13. Is the Christian to obey the state even when the state commands him to do wrong? Can Christians become involved in the overthrow of governments? If so, under what conditions?

What do you think is the main intent of this Romans 13 teaching?

3. Romans 14, 15 is one of Scripture's most significant passages on Christian living. Using principles and attitudes taught here, tell how the following situations might be resolved. List the principles, and explain carefully how they are applied.

Situation 1 Linda's children are in school now, and she wants to go back to work. Her husband, Jim, is opposed. He feels that it's a man's place to earn the family living and that Linda should find fulfillment in her role as a wife and mother. Each feels very strongly about the situation, and each goes back to Scripture to suggest that he or she is right.

Situation 2 Bob has spoken up in his Sunday school class to express his doubts about Scripture's inspiration. He can see the Bible as the history of man's search after God, but not as God's revelation to man. Charlie Dobbs sees this is a basic doctrine, absolutely critical. He has immediately challenged Bob, and the class had responded to take sides.

185

4. Romans 12—15 describes an aggressive kind of community life rather than a passive one. What can you do to work toward community in your church by reaching out to others in active love?